Arise

A Prophetic Call *for* Women *to* Receive Swords, Mantles and Kingdom Assignments

LARRY SPARKS
& PATRICIA KING

DESTINY IMAGE® PUBLISHERS, INC.

P.O. Box 310, Shippensburg, PA 17257-0310

"Promoting Inspired Lives."

This book and all other Destiny Image and Destiny Image Fiction books are available at Christian bookstores and distributors worldwide.

Cover design by Eileen Rockwell
Interior design by Terry Clifton

For more information on foreign distributors, call 717-532-3040.

Reach us on the Internet: www.destinyimage.com.

ISBN 13 TP: 978-0-7684-4489-6
ISBN 13 eBook: 978-0-7684-4490-2
ISBN 13 HC: 978-0-7684-4491-9
ISBN 13 LP: 978-0-7684-4493-3

For Worldwide Distribution, Printed in the U.S.A.

1 2 3 4 5 6 7 8 / 22 21 20 19 18

DEDICATIONS

PATRICIA KING

Dedicated to God's wonderful women who are arising full of faith, courage, love, grace, and wisdom.

LARRY SPARKS

I dedicate *Arise* to my wife, Mercedes Sparks. When I think of how this message is being lived out on a daily basis, I immediately think of my wife. When we were dating, I'll never forget a conversation we had in a restaurant parking lot. I told her that I was looking for a woman of authority. Right there, I think she knew that—whether or not I recognized it—I was looking for *her*. What an honor to see her arise and take her place as a marketplace leader, innovator, prophetic voice, and all around renaissance woman.

CONTENTS

Introduction

DAUGHTERS, ARISE AND PROPHESY!

ARISE. THIS HAS BEEN THE CALL OF HEAVEN TO THE daughters of God ever since Jesus walked the earth.

He confronted and challenged cultural ideals about women. Their position. Their voice. Their importance. If Jesus is truly the ultimate expression of who Father God is and what He desires (see Col. 1:15; Heb. 1:1-3), I believe a revolutionary invitation toward the daughters of God has been extended for over two thousand years.

The Samaritan woman at the well had a life-changing encounter with personified Living Water, and what happened? In the midst of her sin and shame, Jesus unveiled her eyes to revelation about Himself that was simply stunning. Even though the disciples were clearly challenged by the fact that Jesus was talking to a woman, her response was worth noting. This woman *"left her water jar and went away into town and said to the people, 'Come, see a man who told me all that I ever did. Can this be the Christ?' They went out of the town and were coming to him"* (John 4:28-30). She went and *said to the people*. She didn't just tell the women. She didn't just lead women's Bible studies. She preached Jesus and people starting coming to Him.

The Lord is raising up daughters just like this woman. I see you having profound encounters with the Presence of the Holy Spirit, and out of those encounters you will be compelled to carry the news of this wonderful Jesus and His Kingdom into whatever sphere of influence you have been assigned to.

Consider the fruit of this woman's preaching: *"Many Samaritans from that town believed in him because of the woman's testimony"* (John 4:39). Her testimony broke open an entire of community people to believe in Jesus! *Don't tell me a woman can't preach!*

Consider the women at the empty tomb of Jesus! The first people to herald the good news of Jesus' resurrection were women. Matthew 28 records that Mary Magdalene and the other Mary came to visit the tomb of Jesus. While there, they had a historic supernatural encounter. *A great earthquake. An angel from Heaven descended. The stone was rolled away from the tomb. The guards were overwhelmed by the manifest Presence of God's glory and fell as dead men.* In the midst of these incredible supernatural manifestations,

2

a commission was entrusted to the women present there (see Matt. 28:1-10; Luke 24:10). Consider what happened:

> *But the angel said to the women, "Do not be afraid, for I know that you seek Jesus who was crucified. He is not here, for he has risen, as he said. Come, see the place where he lay. Then go quickly and tell his disciples that he has risen from the dead, and behold, he is going before you to Galilee; there you will see him. See, I have told you"* (Matthew 28:5-7).

Go quickly and tell His disciples that He has risen from the dead! It was the voices of the daughters that first thundered the declaration that Jesus was risen.

This commission has never been revoked, daughter of God. May these words provoke you to announce and release the power of the resurrected Christ in whatever sphere He's called you to.

I prophesy that the voice of the daughters will join with the voice of the sons. And as the church, the Ekkelsia of God, encompasses both the bold prophetic declarations and leadership of both men and women, Joel's prophecy will come to fruition in an accelerated measure!

> *And it shall come to pass afterward, that I will pour out my Spirit on all flesh; your sons and your daughters shall prophesy, your old men shall dream dreams, and your young men shall see visions. Even on the male and female servants in those days I will pour out my Spirit* (Joel 2:28-29).

Peter preached that what Joel prophesied was coming to pass before their eyes on that Day of Pentecost. *"This is what was uttered through the prophet Joel"* (Acts 2:16). Yes, on that day the Spirit of God was released out of an open Heaven. We don't need another Pentecost; what we need to do is become good stewards of the Pentecost we have already received. One key way to do this is to step into the very prophetic word *God Himself* gave concerning the last days—sons and daughters would prophesy, releasing the thunder of God's voice into the earth.

As this happens, I believe we are going to witness an acceleration of *Kingdom come, on earth as it is in Heaven* unlike this planet has ever seen.

So it's time to arise, daughter of God, and take your place in the unfolding of Heaven's prophetic plan for history! You were not born to be a spectator of history. History is not supposed to happen to the church; the church is supposed to *happen* to history. Let it be recorded in the history books concerning this hour that the planet was measurably impacted for the better because of the presence of a people—male and female—who carried the Presence and power of Jesus into every arena under the influence of darkness.

Chapter One

MAN, WOMAN, AND THE MANDATE

So God created human beings in his own
image. In the image of God he created them;
male and female he created them. Then God
blessed them and said, "Be fruitful and
multiply. Fill the earth and govern it."
—GENESIS 1:27-28, NLT

THE ENEMY DOES *NOT* WANT YOU TO READ THIS MESSAGE.
But I declare that the words in this book are intended to
prophesy destiny over you. I believe there is an anointing

on these pages, not just to provide you with information to educate but also, an impartation to activate you to fulfill *your* Kingdom assignment. And I announce from the outset that Kingdom assignments are *not* gender specific! *"There is neither Jew nor Greek, there is neither slave nor free, there is no male and female, for you are all one in Christ Jesus"* (Gal. 3:28).

In fact, the powers of darkness have done everything possible to keep the women of God silent and restrained. The devil knows the supernatural force that will be released as both man and woman stand side by side, shoulder to shoulder, and operate in their God-given authority. Even now, I see a vision of man and woman standing and fighting together, side by side. Masculinity will not be compromised or downgraded as men give place to female leaders; in fact, true masculinity will be solidified as men learn to walk in dominion and authority with the daughters of God.

Let me go a step further. Holy Spirit outpouring is incomplete without both the sons *and* daughters arising to prophesy. In order to understand your assignment and the possibilities that Heaven wants to unleash into the earth as this assignment is fulfilled, it's vital to go back to the beginning. This is where God reveals His original blueprint and gives us a glimpse of what's possible because of the redemptive work of Jesus.

BACK TO THE BEGINNING

Then God said, "Let us make man in our image, after our likeness. And let them have dominion over the fish of the sea and over the birds of the heavens and over the livestock and over all the earth and over every creeping thing that creeps on the earth." So God created man in his own image, in the image of God he created him; male and female he created them (Genesis 1:26-27).

CREATED TO RULE

I want you to pay close attention to the language here, as within this mandate is your assignment. First of all, mankind was created to rule. Mankind is not just male— mankind is *male and female*, according to Genesis 1:27.

You know what you were created to rule over? *Every creeping thing that creeps on the earth*. Remember that in Genesis 3, there was a slithering serpent *creeping* on the earth, enticing mankind to

Kingdom assignments are not gender specific!

abandon and surrender this God-given authority. Satan knew full well that he was such a creeping thing. The devil recognized that, because of God's assignment for mankind, he didn't stand a chance *if* man used this authority against him. In fact, because of God's created tiers of jurisdiction, this once-powerful, beautiful, glorious archangel, Lucifer, was now destined to live firmly pressed under the foot of mankind—male and female. Remember that. Mankind is not just man, but man *and* woman.

Remember what God pronounced over the serpent following the Fall?

> *Because you have done this, cursed are you above all livestock and above all beasts of the field; on your belly you shall go, and dust you shall eat all the days of your life* (Genesis 3:14).

Pay close attention to the language used here: *on your belly you shall go.* Sounds like the serpent, the devil, is a "creeping thing" that creeps on the earth. Where is his rightful place, then? Under the authority and subjection of mankind, those created in the image and likeness of God Almighty. Because of Jesus' legal transaction at Calvary, the Son of Man restored this assignment to mankind, his delegated authority over the planet.

While on earth, Jesus told the disciples, "*Behold, I have given you authority to tread on serpents and scorpions, and over all the power of the enemy, and nothing shall hurt you*" (Luke 10:19). Prior to His ascension back to Heaven, Jesus reminded His followers, "*All authority in heaven and on earth has been given to me*" (Matt. 28:18). Jesus did what was legally necessary to reclaim authority from Satan and provide it to those on earth whom He was apostolically commissioning to *go therefore* and disciple nations.

The assignment of discipling nations cannot be accurately grasped apart from also understanding the assignment to *displace* the powers of darkness that have strongholds in the systems, processes, mindsets, and cultures of these nations. To disciple nations, you must first displace the oppositional forces that are trying to disciple nations with a demonic, counterfeit agenda. Discipling nations is, by default, an assignment that demands enforcing authority through warfare. The fight is fixed, yes. Jesus is victorious, absolutely. However, this victory needs to be enforced by men and women who are operating on the same playing field as the powers of darkness—the earth realm. In order for the people of God to bring the influence of Heaven into their spheres of influence, they must approach the task with a sense of authority—that God Himself has authorized them to displace the powers of darkness in their unique areas of jurisdiction. How does this relate to woman and her assignment to rule?

Holy Spirit outpouring is incomplete without both the sons and daughters arising to prophesy.

The Great Commission was not exclusively given to the first band of apostles or even the first-century church; it's the assignment of God for all believers throughout all of time *until* His second coming. *All believers* includes both men and women. If this commission truly does include women (which it does), this means that women have received the necessary authority and power to displace the forces of darkness and disciple nations.

Women of God, you have been commissioned by Jesus Christ to advance the Kingdom of God into every sphere of society. In other words, you have been saved by the blood of

Jesus and filled with the Spirit of God to *go therefore* into the multiple arenas of society—government, politics, educations, arts and entertainment, media, science, law, etc.—and you have been commissioned to bring the Presence, power, influence, government, and culture of the Kingdom into those places. In an upcoming chapter, Patricia will provide specific strategies on your role in discipling each of the unique spheres of society. You don't belong on the sidelines; you were born for the frontlines!

To disciple nations, you must first displace the oppositional forces that are trying to disciple nations with a demonic, counterfeit agenda.

You don't need to wait until a man acknowledges this assignment in order for you to engage it. Yes, have accountability in your life. Of course, pursue appropriate (*not* domineering or oppressive) spiritual covering and protection from both men and women. That's a given for all believers. But woman of God, you were created to rule. What does this look like? *Displacing* and *discipling.* It looks like *ruling over* and *subduing.* I know there are many people who become uncomfortable with this language of authority. Understand this is not, as it has been misunderstood and manipulated in the past, to suggest that Christians are looking to somehow take over society through violent upheaval. Not at all. There is spiritual violence for sure as we impose the Kingdom of God, but it plays out on the unseen battleground of the heavenly realm. And the violence that accompanies spiritual warfare is not aimed at displacing people; it's aimed at displacing darkness that is having a destructive influence on the people occupying those unique spheres of culture.

ASK FOR THE NATIONS

I will declare the decree: The Lord has said to Me, "You are My Son, today I have begotten You. Ask of Me, and I will give You the nations for Your inheritance, and the ends of the earth for Your possession" (Psalm 2:7-8, NKJV).

What does this prophetic passage look like fleshed out in your life today?

And Jesus came and said to them, "All authority in heaven and on earth has been given to me. Go therefore and make disciples of all nations, baptizing them in the name of the Father and of the Son and of the Holy Spirit" (Matthew 28:18-19).

Consider the relationship between Psalm 2:7-8 and Mathew 28:18-19. I don't know how conversations take place within the Trinity, but somehow David was able to tune in to this divine exchange within the counsel of the Lord as we see captured in Psalm 2. The Father says to Jesus, His Son, *ask of Me, and I will give You the nations.* I believe the manifestation of Jesus' *asking* for the nations takes place as He gives the Great Commission in Matthew 28.

- God created man and woman (mankind). He placed man and woman in the Garden to rule, using the authority He entrusted to them.
- Man willingly surrendered that authority *to* the devil.
- The Son of Man willingly reclaimed that authority *from* the devil through His atonement and resurrection.
- Now, just prior to His ascending back to Heaven, the Son of Man gives the "sons (and daughters) of man" a commission that basically says: *Go forth in My authority and power and give Me the nations!*

Where does Matthew 28 say anything about authority and power being transferred to you and me? It doesn't. However, Mark 16 reveals, very clearly, that Jesus was giving both His power and His authority to redeemed mankind to reclaim the nations for Him.

Just before the ascension, Jesus announces, "*But you shall receive power when the Holy Spirit has come upon you; and you shall be witnesses to Me in Jerusalem, and in all Judea and Samaria, and to the end of the earth*" (Acts 1:8, NKJV).

Power to do what? Jesus clarifies this commission all the more through Mark's account:

Go into all the world and preach the gospel to every creature. He who believes and is baptized will be saved; but he who does not believe will be condemned. And these signs will follow those who believe: In My name they will cast out demons; they will speak with new tongues; they will take up serpents; and if they drink anything deadly, it will by no means hurt them; they will lay hands on the sick, and they will recover (Mark 16:15-18).

Woman of God, you were born for this moment in history to *ask for the nations!*

PROPHETIC WORD: ASK FOR YOUR MOUNTAIN!

I prophesy over you that you will no longer look to the left or the right, desiring to be called like "her" or "him." Arise in your present assignment and embrace it. Yes, there is "glory to glory." Of course there is promotion, but the Lord looks at how you steward your present moment and assignment to determine qualification for advancement and promotion. Where are the Kingdom women who would arise in His strength, here and now, to be good stewards of their present assignments? Don't dismiss this present assignment, for it may not look like "nations" right now, but rest assured, nations are being born in how you steward where you are. Everyone wants to get to the next place—the next level. But the Lord refuses to allow passage to this next dimension until we can witness a people who have the character, the integrity, and the ability to steward the glory of the next place. This is cultivated in the "present place." Likewise, where are the daughters who would ask the Holy Spirit for a mountain? *Ask for a mountain,* says the Lord.

Ask for the mountain that causes your heart to burn.

Caleb asked for a mountain at 80 years old (see Josh. 14:6-15). For the Lord would say to you, woman of God, *ask for the mountain that causes your heart to burn.* Ask for the mountain of influence that produces in you the greatest frustration—your greatest irritation. Ask for the mountain that you sense the Spirit is giving you solutions for. It's normal human reaction to feel some level of burden or irritation over different issues and problems in the world; it's the sign of a Kingdom assignment to actually be divinely entrusted with the solutions that could bring transformation to those areas of crisis and dysfunction.

Many believers sadly wrestle with their positioning in time. *Why was I born in this time period?* They think it would have been better living back in the time of Jesus, or back in the "good old days" (whenever those were). There have never really been "good old days." And plus, you were not called and anointed and empowered for comfort; you were called to run toward the conflict and crisis. Woman of God, there is something in you that provokes you to toward injustice. That something is a Someone called Holy Spirit. He is God, and God cannot stand injustice. The woman of God runs toward oppression. She runs toward brokenness. You were filled with the Spirit, not to wish for a more comfortable time in history to live in, but to cooperate with God inside of you to release His Kingdom, His reign, His justice, His solutions, His strategies, His healing, and His liberating power into the hopeless situations you're being con-fronted with *today*.

This starts in whatever sphere of influence you have been called to. Nations are not just countries or con-tinents or people groups; *nations* include systems, cul-tures, and thought processes. Nations are shaped through the Kingdom of God having a direct, measurable impact on how people think, do life, conduct business, express art, govern, lead, etc.

> *You were not called and anointed and empowered for comfort; you were called to run toward the conflict and crisis.*

Ask for your nation! Ask the Holy Spirit to show you a sphere of influence He is calling you to. Most likely, this will be an arena or subject you have passion, talent, and aptitude for. Dr. Lance Wallnau explains that, often, the area of your greatest passion is usually the area where you have the most frustration; you're frustrated at the level of darkness that has had influence over that particular sphere. You want to effect change. You want to bring Heaven's wisdom and strategy. You want to release solutions and innovation. And yes, you also want to displace the powers of darkness that have held sway in that sphere of influence. That is a legal desire, as you were created to rule over and subdue the darkness!

It's time to arise and step into your Genesis 1 mandate: "*Be fruitful and multiply. Fill the earth and govern it*" (Gen. 1:28, NLT). Jesus made it possible, once again, for mankind to have a governing voice in the earth over the *creeping one*, the devil. And remember, mankind is not just men; it's men and women.

PRAYERS AND DECREES

Father, I pray you would open my eyes through the work of the Holy Spirit. Show me how I was created to operate in authority—Your delegated authority—over everything that creeps on the earth. I recognize Satan is a defeated angelic being who operates in the earth realm. He is a creeping thing upon the earth, and therefore I have authority and dominion over the devil and his forces of darkness.

I renounce and reject the counterfeit feminist movement that has sought to displace men. I declare that, Holy Spirit, what You are doing in the earth is not about displacing or replacing the sons—it's about joining sons and daughters together. It's about Your men and women rising up together to exercise Your dominion on earth.

I decree that I am called to release Heaven's dominion on earth. *I recognize that Heaven's dominion is not overthrowing things in the natural; it's about displacing the powers of darkness that have influence in the spirit realm. Because I am in Christ and Christ is in me, I have His authority. It's not my own; it's the authority of Jesus entrusted to me. May I use His authority like He would use it. May I be so linked with Jesus, through the Holy Spirit, that I pray like He would pray. I speak as He would speak. I respond to problems the way Jesus would.*

Arise Reflection

KAREN WHEATON

LOOKING BACK, I HAVE TO SMILE WHEN I REMEMBER HOW my dad was always a bit concerned my mother was going to be a "woman preacher." Actually, mother never felt called to "preach" from a pulpit. But, oh, the message she preached every day from her life! It so deeply impacted my sister and me that both of us became women preachers!

Now, after 40 years of full-time ministry, I marvel at the journey. My heart is warmed when I recall the night God called me to work with the youth of this generation. I explained to Him why I was not the best choice for the job—I was too old, not cool, and too busy in the ministry. However, I discovered God is not concerned with our age, our "coolness," our schedule, or our gender. His searching eyes are simply looking for a willing heart that will answer His call with a trusting, "Yes."

God has given each of us, male and female, a purpose for being on the earth. We have been given gifts and abilities to walk in the fullness of that purpose. As believers in Christ, Satan knows he has lost us to eternity in Heaven, so the next best thing he can do is steal or destroy our purpose. He has worked especially hard through the misinterpretation of Scripture to silence the voices of women. This indicates how much he fears what is coming out of our mouths! He has worked through fear and intimidation to cause women to feel inadequate to walk with boldness and confidence in their purpose. But for you and me, his plan has failed.

The Holy Spirit is bringing fresh revelation to the church concerning His desire for His daughters. This amazing book, *Arise*, is one of the ways He is revealing the truth of His heart! I believe we are in the "last days" that Joel spoke of, and it is time for sons and daughters to prophesy! There is nothing Satan fears more than the power and authority that is in the Word!

Woman of God, open your mouth and prophesy! What does it mean to prophesy? It means to declare the word and will of God. We don't have to have a pulpit to prophesy. As ambassadors of God, everywhere we go we are speaking to circumstances, places, and people, calling them into the will of our Father!

In our prayer closets, we are moving angels and casting out demons by the power of His Word! As intercessors, we boldly lift our voices and call our prodigals home!

Second Timothy 4:2 was written to *all* of us, male and female alike: *"Preach the word; be ready in season and out of season; reprove, rebuke, and exhort, with complete patience and teaching."*

So from one "woman preacher" to another—your voice matters! Your purpose is now! With no more excuses and no time to waste, run boldly into all that God has destined for you!

Chapter Two

ARISE AND FULFILL
END-TIMES PROPHECY

And in the last days it shall be, God declares,
that I will pour out my Spirit on all flesh,
and your sons and your daughters shall
prophesy, and your young men shall see visions,
and your old men shall dream dreams.
—ACTS 2:17

WHEN IT COMES TO THE TOPIC OF "END-TIMES" EVENTS, it's so easy to veer off into speculation. We have our elaborate charts, pictorial graphs, and detailed, carefully plotted timelines of how we expect everything should play out. Even though there is much to debate about concerning the specifics of how the end of the age will unfold, there is one sure prophetic word that we should be focusing on more if we want to effectively partner with God's *last days* purposes (and by the way, we have been in the *last days* since Jesus left the planet and the Spirit descended at Pentecost).

In Acts 2:17, the apostle Peter is basically saying to the group gathered: "What you are presently seeing and experiencing is Joel's Old Testament prophecy coming to pass. This day marks the beginning of the promised outpouring of the Spirit, and *these* are some of the evidences and signs that we are experiencing this prophesied outpouring."

> *One of the key signs of the last days outpouring is sons and daughters prophesying together.*

One of the key signs of the *last days* outpouring is *sons and daughters* prophesying together. What does this mean? Men and women, boys and girls hearing and boldly declaring the Word of the Lord. In many ways, this is a restoration of what God envisioned in the Garden. To have perspective on where God is taking things in the future, it's vital to return, once again, to the beginning.

THE DOMINION MANDATE AND HOLY SPIRIT OUTPOURING

In the Garden of Eden, we caught a glimpse of God's dominion mandate, which involved both men and women ruling the earth side by side. The powers of darkness will never be brought under the subjection that God desires until man and woman rule *together*. Reconsider the *Dominion Mandate* of the Lord, presented specifically to both man and woman: *"And God blessed them. And God said to them, 'Be fruitful and multiply and fill the earth and subdue it, and have dominion over the fish of the sea and over the birds of the heavens and over every living thing that moves on the earth'"* (Gen. 1:28).

This verse sets the tone for this entire teaching, as the original will and intent of God is revealed right here. Pay close attention to the language and context of this Scripture. First, look at the *context*.

God gives this commission before the Fall of mankind, at which point humanity willingly surrendered authority of the planet over to Satan. In other words, what God was proposing to both man and woman was truly His *perfect will*, as everything in Eden was considered good and *very good* by the Maker Himself. So, what's the perfect will of God plainly revealed? Look no further than what's described in those first two chapters of Genesis, prior to sin's entrance and subsequent contamination of created order.

The earth began in a garden and will *conclude* with a garden. Look at Revelation 22:1-5 and compare it to the original environment described in the Garden of Eden.

Then the angel showed me the river of the water of life, bright as crystal, flowing from the throne of God and of the Lamb through the middle of the street of the city; also, on either side of the river, the tree of life with its twelve kinds of fruit, yielding its fruit each month. The leaves of the tree were for the healing of the nations. No longer will there be anything accursed, but the throne of God and of the Lamb will be in it, and his servants will worship him. They will see his face, and his name will be on their foreheads. And night will be no more. They will need no light of lamp or sun, for the Lord God will be their light, and they will reign forever and ever (Revelation 22:1-5).

Second, look at the *dominion language* in Genesis 1:28. God is intentional with what He says. After all, He both declares and *is* the Word. If *the Word* is literally the name that God assigns to Himself, what He speaks must carry significant weight. This is a "no brainer," in theory, but it calls us to reconsider some of the portions of Scripture that we quickly pass over. In Genesis 1:28, the call to *rule* was given to *them*. Not *him*—them!

God blessed *them*.

God said to *them*.

The assignment to have dominion and governance was not gender-specific; it was directed at both man and woman. Although this dominion was surrendered to Satan in the Garden of Eden because of sin, I believe it was restored because of Calvary.

DOMINION OVER THE FORCES OF DARKNESS

What does this Kingdom dominion look like today? It's not Christians taking over society, turning nations into theocracies. Rather, it's believers taking authority in the spirit realm so that society benefits from the peace that comes through the prayers, intercessions, and yes, even the presence of Christ-followers, filled with the Holy Spirit.

It's about serving mankind by dealing with his enemy. It's about creating environments where those who are filled with the Spirit have spiritual jurisdiction in the airways *so that* those who are disconnected from God can be introduced to Him. It's about confronting the ills that try to *steal, kill,* and *destroy* from humanity and dealing with them by enforcing the authority of Jesus' name and releasing the power of the Spirit. The believer's authority is aimed at demonic powers in the heavenly places that either have, or seek to have, strongholds in society. There is still a devil on planet earth who operates both legally and illegally. He operates legally when authority is *given* to him through agreement, sin, divination, witchcraft, rebellion, the occult, and other means of human partnership. Paul describes this as giving *"the devil a foothold"* (Eph. 4:27, NIV). People partner with the devil through their thoughts, belief systems, actions, and agreements. Peter addresses him as our adversary who *"prowls around like a roaring lion, seeking someone to devour"* (1 Pet. 5:8). He is looking for someone who is devour-able. Typically, such a person has positioned themselves to be prey for the devil through giving him some kind of foothold or place in their lives.

Also, in true form to his nature, the devil functions *illegally*. In John 8:44, Jesus explains that the devil "*was a murderer from the beginning, and does not stand in the truth, because there is no truth in him. When he lies, he speaks out of his own character, for he is a liar and the father of lies.*" If all Satan does is lie, I can guarantee you, he does not deal with mankind fairly. In this capacity, he is operating as Jesus describes in John 10:10: "*The thief comes only to steal and kill and destroy. I came that they may have life and have it abundantly.*"

When the sons and daughters of God exercise their dominion today, it should look similar to what God envisioned for Adam and Eve in the Garden.

> *Then God said, "Let Us make man in Our image, according to Our likeness; let them have dominion over the fish of the sea, over the birds of the air, and over the cattle, over all the earth and over every creeping thing that creeps on the earth"* (Genesis 1:26, NKJV).

One of the *creeping things* upon the earth was the former archangel Lucifer, now the serpent Satan. We have already been introduced to this concept, but it is worth repeating. He was placed *under* the authority of mankind— well, he should have been. We know what took place. Adam and Eve gave away their authority through sin, Jesus won it back through redemption, and now that same mandate to be a people who *tread upon* that creeping one, Satan, should be in effect. Jesus said, "*Look, I have given you authority over all the power of the enemy, and you can walk among snakes and scorpions and crush them. Nothing will injure you"* (Luke 10:19, NLT).

True Kingdom dominion looks like the powers of darkness being subdued by a victorious, Spirit-filled church. This is the church that Paul describes in Ephesians 1. I encourage you to read through the entire chapter, particularly focusing on verses 21 through 23 when it comes to the identity and assignment of the church.

Paul describes the place of Jesus and His authority as *"far above all rule and authority and power and dominion, and above every name that is named, not only in this age but also in the one to come"* (Eph. 1:21). While this is awe-inspiring concerning the Son of God, it is also an invitation to the people of God who have been called the *body of Christ*. Review Jesus' placement of authority for a moment and then consider your role in it.

> *And he put all things under his feet and gave him as head over all things to the church, which is his body, the fullness of him who fills all in all* (Ephesians 1:22-23).

Jesus was raised to a place of authority that is infinitely superior to all powers of darkness in this age and in the age to come. What does Paul call the church? *His body* (see Eph. 1:23; 1 Cor. 12:27). Jesus is the head, but you and I are His body. We are the extension of Jesus in the earth, which means we ought to be doing what *His body* would do. When Jesus walked the earth, what did *His body do*? Laid hands on the sick and brought healing. Raised the dead. Cast out demons and delivered people from torment. He touched the untouchable. He reached into the dirt of depravity and raised people out of their sin. Jesus' physical body on earth was intent on revealing the nature, character, personality and will of Father God. One of the ways this was expressed was through confrontation with powers that were oppositional to God's nature being revealed. This is why John described Jesus' assignment as such: "*The reason the Son of God appeared was to destroy the works of the devil*" (1 John 3:8). The works of the devil were the ills and sorrows wrought by human sin that since the Garden of Eden had prevented people from knowing and experiencing the Father. Jesus was on a mission, and just before He left the planet He made sure that you and I knew that our mission was to continue His mission: "*As the Father has sent me, even so I am sending you*" (John 20:21). After making this statement, He "*breathed on them and said to them, 'Receive the Holy Spirit'*" (John 20:22).

At this moment, everything shifted. At this point, Jesus had made salvation available, which was accompanied by the infilling of the Spirit (Spirit baptism came later on the Day of Pentecost). The implications here are outstanding for every single born-again believer, male and female. If you are saved, or born again, or have received Jesus as Lord and Savior—or whatever language we use to describe the supernatural translation from darkness to light that we undergo at conversion—then you, a mortal human being, have been positioned to operate with the same advantage Jesus Himself had when He victoriously confronted the devil during His wilderness temptation.

What silenced Satan every single time? An anointed declaration. A statement. A *voice of prophetic authority*. What will silence Satan today, destroying his works

and revoking the dark forces that are bent on preventing the world from seeing the Father? *A prophetic voice
that boldly answers the powers of darkness by declaring
it is written.*

DOMINION THROUGH THE DECLARED PROPHETIC VOICE OF SONS AND DAUGHTERS

Using Luke 4 as our text, Jesus models how both men and
women should deal with the powers of darkness. Some
might respond, *yeah, but that was Jesus—the Son of God.
Surely we cannot follow His example when it comes to dealing
with the devil. He was God, after all.* Yes, Jesus was and is
God. He never took a vacation from being God. He never
graduated to God-status. He didn't earn it. He didn't work
for it. Jesus was, is, and ever will be God. In the wilderness,
Jesus was God. And yet, He made a decision to overcome
the devil like a human being could, thus giving all Spirit-
filled people a model to follow. (Remember, immediately
before the temptation, Jesus was filled with the Spirit at
His baptism.)

You are filled with the same Holy Spirit that Jesus had
in the wilderness. You know what else? You have access to
the same *Word of God* that Jesus had too! The word of God
gave Jesus prophetic authority to silence every temptation
of the devil. In the same manner, you have authority to
make prophetic decrees, cancelling the works of the devil
and releasing the purposes of God. What authorizes you
to operate in prophetic authority? The Word of God.

The devil said to him, "If you are the Son of God, command this stone to become bread." And Jesus answered him, "It is written, 'Man shall not live by bread alone'" (Luke 4:3-4).

Jesus was careful to answer the devil with the very words of God. Likewise, you can operate in this same Kingdom authority to the degree that you decree what *God has already declared.* You do not have authority to "name and claim" whatever you feel like. Such a perverse, self-seeking approach has given birth to the carnal prosperity message. This is truly an aberration and a demonic distraction from the authentic prophetic power that God wants to release through His people. You must follow Jesus' example and say what the Father is saying: *"For I have not spoken on my own authority, but the Father who sent me has himself given me a commandment—what to say and what to speak"* (John 12:49). Once again, Jesus provides a model to follow. Because of His intimacy with the Father, He could hear the words that were first spoken in Heaven and purposed to be released into the earth. Jesus cherished the Scriptures. His model invites us into the same dimension of intimacy with Father God, the offspring of which will be a prophetic Kingdom authority that binds hell and looses Heaven.

Prophetic authority means we say what God is saying. This is what happens when you declare the Word. We've so grievously softened this, simply describing it as quoting Scripture. To say what God is saying means we are functioning in the prophetic capacity the Holy Spirit opened up to all believers.

At this point you might be asking, *where do women fit into all of this?* I promise, we are getting there. The church *should be* doing what Jesus did in the wilderness, speaking with the same authority and power that establishes Kingdom realities in the earth. The body of Christ should be known for the volume of its power, not the loudness of its obnoxiousness.

Because we have often failed to operate in this prophetic identity, we've become known for our loudness—an obnoxious, condemning, judgmental, against-everybody-and-everything loudness. Often, the church is either a laughingstock or object of ridicule because it's seen as a community of kill-joys. We're known for everything and everyone we're against. Sadly, we even become associated with fringe groups that completely misrepresent Jesus. I'm not saying we shouldn't have a moral voice in the earth; we should. We have something to say concerning morality, sin, social issues, injustice, and all manner of cultural ills. The church really

Instead of being known for pointing a finger of condemnation against people, Jesus' church should be recognized as a community that points a finger of Kingdom power against the forces of darkness.

should be functioning as the conscience of society. Martin Luther King, Jr. so eloquently explained how the church should be operating in its moral capacity: "The church must be reminded that it is not the master or the servant of the state, but rather the conscience of the state. It must be the guide and the critic of the state, and never its tool. If the church does not recapture its prophetic zeal, it will become an irrelevant social club without moral or spiritual authority."[1]

Pay attention to Dr. King's final comments, though. "If the church does not recapture its prophetic zeal, it will become an irrelevant social club without moral or spiritual authority." We cannot be loud with our protest signs and moral outcries and yet be powerless when it comes to serving the very humanity that Jesus came to seek and save. We serve humanity *not* by first pointing a condemning finger but, instead, by modeling Jesus who released the *finger of God*. The finger of God was not one of condemnation, but as we see in the Scriptures it was one of healing, deliverance, and supernatural demonstration! *"But if it is by the finger of God that I cast out demons, then the kingdom of God has come upon you"* (Luke 11:20).

Instead of being known for pointing a finger of condemnation against people, Jesus' church should be recognized as a community that points a finger of Kingdom power against the forces of darkness. It's only as the bride of Christ is operating in her spiritual authority that her words concerning morality and social ills will have greater weight.

For the church to be a community functioning in prophetic power, both the sons and daughters need to arise and speak together. The voice of the Ekklesia cannot be divided. It certainly cannot be undergoing internal division. Remember, a kingdom divided cannot stand (see Mark 3:24). Furthermore, a kingdom operating in division cannot stand, advance *or* occupy. This goes for both the kingdom of Satan and the Kingdom of God. As long as certain members of the body of Christ try to mute the prophetic voice of the daughters, then the collective impact of the church will be muted compared to what it could be.

AMPLIFYING THE CHURCH'S VOLUME

The church's volume will amplify to the degree that both sons and daughters are given an equal voice to declare the decree of the Lord.

How did Jesus overcome the enemy in His wilderness temptation? He did *not* overthrow Satan by wielding His divine "God powers." Jesus could have, though. In that moment, while He was weak in the flesh through fasting, He could have drawn from His identity as God and completely wiped out the devil with one fiery breath from His mouth (see 2 Thess. 2:8). He did not. Why? One reason, I believe, was because in the wilderness temptation— at the height of experiencing the pain, tiredness and weariness of His humanity—the Son of God was extending a model to the sons (and daughters) of men on how to enforce their authority over the serpent.

The church's volume will amplify to the degree that both sons and daughters are given an equal voice to declare the decree of the Lord.

What does Joel's prophecy announce about what will take place in the *last days?* *"Your sons and your daughters shall prophesy"* (Joel 2:28).

It's vital that the daughters of God have a voice and that this voice is championed by the body of Christ. This is a key manifestation of how the church is destined to operate in authority and power, sons and daughters declaring the decree of the Lord together. This is the prophetic in operation. When both the sons and daughters are prophesying together, I believe Jesus' vision for the church in Matthew 16 can come to pass:

> *I will build My church; and the gates of Hades will not overpower it. I will give you the keys of the kingdom of heaven; and whatever you bind on earth shall have been bound in heaven, and whatever you loose on earth shall have been loosed in heaven"* (Matthew 16:18-19, NASB).

What is one of the primary ways through which things are *bound* and *loosed?* The prophetic decree. Without men and women operating in their prophetic authority, loosing what Heaven declares as lawful and binding what Heaven forbids, I am convinced we will not see God's end-time prophecy fulfilled of *all flesh* experiencing the outpouring of the Holy Spirit. To see the cry of God's heart come to pass, it's time for "all hands on deck."

This is why the enemy seeks to *silence* the voice of the daughters. For the thunder of God to be heard, the voices of the sons and daughters need to be prophesying in unity, declaring the wonderful works of the Lord. The earth is just waiting for one voice that emerges, confronting the powers of darkness with the prophetic decree of *it is written*. Remember, Jesus didn't defeat the devil in the wilderness using His God-power; He overcame the devil making declarations of the Word. He was saying what His Father had already said. As He did this, surely a sword was swinging in the invisible realm, bringing to naught each attempt of the devil. Just imagine the power that is waiting to be unlocked as the sword of the Lord is fully extended through a church where both sons and daughters prophesy, boldly declaring what the Father has *already said* concerning the injustice, the sickness, the poverty, the racial tension, the upheaval, the depression, the fear, and the forces of darkness that are trying maintain their occupancy on planet earth. These strongholds must break at the thunder of the prophetic of the Lord! Consider what happens as this voice thunders forth:

> *The voice of the Lord is over the waters; the God of glory thunders, the Lord, over many waters. The voice of the Lord is powerful; the voice of the Lord is full of majesty. The voice of the Lord breaks the cedars; the Lord breaks the cedars of Lebanon. He makes Lebanon to skip like a calf, and Sirion like a young wild ox. The voice of the Lord flashes forth flames of fire. The voice of the Lord shakes the wilderness; the Lord shakes the wilderness of Kadesh. The voice of the Lord makes the deer give birth and strips the forests bare, and in his temple all cry, "Glory!"* (Psalm 29:3-9)

Arise

In Psalm 29, David paints an Old Testament picture of what happens in the natural realm when the voice of the Lord goes forth. Imagine the level of impact that this same voice has now, not booming out of the heavens but thundering out of the mouths of sons and daughters filled with the Spirit?

NOTE

1. Martin Luther King and Coretta Scott King, *Strength to Love* (Minneapolis, MN: Fortress, 2010), 59.

Chapter Three

THE LIBRARY OF UNFULFILLED PROPHETIC WORDS

*A prophetic word is a Heaven-to-earth
invitation to partnership. God, in His
sovereignty, gives promises and prophetic
words to humanity. Humanity is responsible
for stewarding these words unto fulfillment.*

COULD IT BE THAT THERE ARE PROPHETIC WORDS WAIT-
ing to be fulfilled by those who believe they are unqualified

to step into the assignments that have been prophesied over them?

Even now, I sense that as you read these words, the Spirit of God is bringing to your remembrance promises and prophecies, dreams and visions, ambitions and desires from past seasons. *Remembrance and resurrection,* says the Lord. He's bringing things to your remembrance that He wants to resurrect. Yes, there are things that God doesn't want you to do. Yes, there is such a thing as selfish, carnal ambition. Yet I am convinced that because many women fear these things, they lay the possibility of stepping into such assignments down without the clear direction of the Lord. Or, they assume that if the Lord asks them to lay something down, that thing is gone and lost forever.

I hear it now, as I type these words, the Lord is bringing to your remembrance things He wants to resurrect for *His glory.* You fulfilling your assignment is not about building a career or brand. It's not about making your name great. If that's your driving ambition, then yes, God will most likely ask you to lay that thing down. And just because your ambition might be off, it does not mean that the object of your desire is wrong. It just means the Holy Spirit has some maturing work to do on your heart. We have all been there, and trust me, we don't want to be promoted beyond our heart's ability to carry the weight of what we are promoted into.

And yet, on the flipside, there is a library in the spirit of unfulfilled prophecies that are just waiting for your agreement. They are waiting for a man, woman, child—someone—who will say "Yes" with their lives to what

God is inviting them into. More about this in the pages ahead. Right now, I want to share why I am so passionate about helping you fulfill your assignment.

WHY IS THIS IMPORTANT?—MY STORY

You may be asking, *why do you, Larry—a guy—have such a passion to see women take their place in ministry, leadership, and fulfilling their assignments in the Kingdom of God?* Good question. Let me explain briefly, so I can give you context for what the Lord is doing in the earth.

When I first encountered the Holy Spirit back in 1999, I received a profound touch by His Presence—a touch I didn't have language for. That is, until I started listening to worship leader Darlene Zschech (Australia-based songwriter of "Shout to the Lord," "The Potter's Hand," and "Victor's Crown" among many worship classics) and ultimately attended a night of worship she led in Fort Lauderdale, FL back in May of 2000. I received a life-changing impartation that night. She didn't pray for me. I didn't get touched and fall down under the power. None of that. But I'll never forget the internal conversations going on in my head that evening, as I experienced wave after wave of the manifest, tangible Presence of God. It was so strong, there were moments I didn't think my physical body could contain it. I was effectively ruined for anything less than a life-pursuit of *that* Presence. The point? That hunger was, I believe, a transferable impartation that was released from Darlene to me in that atmosphere—a desperately hungry teenager simply wanting to know and experience the living God.

In addition, I was searching for practical advice on how to live the Christian life. I had been bogged down with religious legalism from my elementary and middle school years, attending a very strict Christian school. I wanted enough of God to make it to Heaven (and not get "left behind" at the rapture). How much of God was that? *Not very much.* Once I tasted and saw He was good through my encounter in His Presence, I sought out those who would disciple me on my new journey of walking with Jesus. One of the most profound, steadfast, and consistent voices in my life (and, I am certain, millions of lives worldwide) has been Joyce Meyer. A woman. I didn't care. I repeat, gender is irrelevant when it comes to the anointing of the Spirit upon you and the assignment of God for you. The impact of these women on my life was so profound, actually, that it shaped the way I prayed for my future spouse. I literally prayed for a woman of authority, like Joyce Meyer, who spoke her mind, was bold, and had her own unique calling and assignment. I have received this gift a million times over in my beautiful wife, Mercedes.

It never dawned upon me that women often received inferior treatment by the church and in the church, let alone society. I was insulated from this reality until I actually started talking about these things and experienced significant resistance. Sadly, some of the strongest resistance I experienced concerning women in leadership/authority came from other women. My peers. I believe many have bought into a demonic lie purposed to restrain them from fulfilling destiny. *No more.* Even though I've had some incredible spiritual mentors and leaders who were men, it was many of the women of God who had a profound, formative impact on my life and significantly influenced my quest for the Holy Spirit. Daughters of God, it's time for you to *arise!*

GOD IS SANCTIFYING CAREER AMBITION

I want to share a prophetic vision the Lord gave me, a biblical example, and then a charge for you, daughter of God, to dramatically reconsider this idea of "career ambition." Sadly, in the church world this form of ambition has been considered to be carnal, worldly, sinful, and especially distasteful—let alone for a woman. After all, for a woman to be driven by career ambition, with a desire to ascend the "corporate ladder" of influence, has been considered taboo. What makes career ambition sinful is *not* the act of gaining influence, wealth, or affluence; it's the heart that drives and motivates the process. We can no longer say a sweeping, black-and-white "No" to the women of God rising to take their Kingdom position in the marketplace. Rather, we need to partner with God to see the Holy Spirit's wind blow the dust off of Kingdom assignments that are awaiting agreement in the earth realm. Again, amplification of the Ekklesia's impact on society will take place in proportion to both men and women, sons and daughters, leading together. These assignments are not awarded based on gender; rather, they are given to anyone who will say an all-out, all-in "Yes" to King Jesus.

THE VISION OF THE OLD DUSTY BOOKS

In a vision, the Lord showed me a room—it looked like a library—containing bookshelves that were filled with ancient-looking, dusty volumes. I sensed that these books contained promises or prophetic words that people have chosen to "shelve."

Sometimes, when people receive a "too good to be true" promise from the Lord, or a dream from Heaven, or an outrageous prophetic word (it may confront their minds, but it's in agreement with the Word of God and rings true to the recipient's spirit), their initial response is *not* agreement. It's "I'm going to put this on the *shelf* for another season."

Yes, God is sovereign, and He works in His ordained times and seasons. This is absolutely true, and furthermore I believe trying to manufacture the fulfillment of a dream, promise, or prophetic word *outside* of the appointed times of the Lord is dangerous at worst and intensely frustrating at best. So keep that in mind.

Here is the problem, though. Many people—and this is especially true for the daughters of God—receive legitimate words and directives from Heaven. However, these words will not automatically come to pass. Many live perpetually disappointed with God because, day after day, they are increasingly aware of unfulfilled prophetic words and unanswered prayers. Again, God *is* sovereign and He operates in times and seasons. At the same time, Jesus doesn't offer a lot of contingency theology for unanswered prayers. In the Gospels. I encourage you to study Jesus' approach to prayer. *Ask. Seek. Knock.* Every time Jesus coaches His disciples in prayer, He always presents prayer in a context where *answers* were the end result. So, why don't we see more answers? Ironically, I don't have *all the answers* to this question. One thing, though, that I sense and I want to provoke you with is this thought—unanswered prayer and unfulfilled prophecy might just be waiting for a response from someone in the earth realm. They demand partnership. And yet, what happens if we are "shelving" prophetic words that demand spiritual pondering that leads to partnering and thus manifests through fulfillment? Prophetic words need to be partnered with. Track with me here for a moment.

THE PROCESS OF YOUR PROMISE

I repeat, not every word you receive is meant to come to fruition immediately. In fact, most often, prophetic words call the recipients into a process of becoming a person who can actually shoulder the weightiness of the word received. Make sense? Anyone can receive a prophetic word, regardless of what state they are in. I believe the Lord delights in sharing words with those who are going in a completely opposite direction to His desired path for their lives. Why? A prophetic word is a confrontational call to do a sanctified "about face." You're moving in one direction—often pretty adamantly. The Lord then sovereignly speaks right into your mess. Into your rebellion. Into your selfishness. Into your sin. You didn't earn it. You certainly didn't deserve it. That's often the nature of a prophetic word or promise from God—He delivers these from Heaven to earth, often through human vessels, sovereignly.

Through the word, the Lord doesn't necessarily say, "Hey, you've got to get your act together because I can't use you in this messy condition." And God has a right to say things like that. He does chasten and discipline those He loves (see Prov. 3:12; Heb. 12:6). I'm just saying that often, a prophetic word that gives someone a supernatural glimpse of who they are meant to be and what they are called to do actually summons them to rise above the sin that is entangling and ensnaring them in their present season (see Heb. 12:1-2). And more often than not, He delivers a word of destiny. It's confrontational, sure, but not because God decides to rub your face in your error. It confronts your error and sin because you are given a glimpse of the *greatness* that God has prepared for you. Yes, greatness. Not *your* greatness—God's greatness. You are made to carry, represent and release the greatness of God. When we are reminded of this reality, lesser things and inferior pleasures are exposed for the sham they are.

Prophetic words are, in fact, previews and glimpses of what Paul writes about in Ephesians 2:10, those "*good works, which God prepared beforehand, that we should walk in them.*"

But here is the crux. Just receiving a prophetic word does not guarantee the word will come to pass. God delivers the word to you sovereignly, in whatever form *He* decides.

In the process of partnering with a prophetic word, the Spirit of God cultivates within you capacity through character. He wants you to have the character to walk in the reality that was announced to you in seed form, delivered through a prophetic word, vision, dream, promise from Scripture, etc. Simply put, the church would see more happen as she continues to shift her emphasis from being me-centered to God-centered. God is not looking for perfect people. Your personal striving for perfection doesn't position you to be more qualified to see promises and prophecies fulfilled. Do you know what does? A heart that's bent toward God's agenda for the ages coming to pass. What is this? *"Indeed, as I live, all the earth will be filled with the glory of the Lord"* (Num. 14:21, NASB).

GOD'S AGENDA FOR THE AGES

The earth will be filled with His glory as sons and daughters actually receive the inheritance that the Father promised the Son. I believe the church is the instrument—the vehicle and the body—through which the Son of God will receive His inheritance of the nations. This will surely not happen as women are deceived into believing the only place they belong in the church is the women's ministry, or children's ministry, or nursery. Furthermore, this will not happen as long as women are told that career ambition is sinful and that their desire for advancement is carnal. Going further still, this will not happen as men and women, filled with the Spirit of God, mistakenly believe that ministry *in* the church is actually building the church. Ministry in the church context maintains the church community, yes, and is valuable service no doubt. But for the earth to be filled with glory and for the Son of God to receive nations, I propose that the church needs to rethink its strategy. The driving narrative from the pulpit cannot be "serve in the church" but, rather, *serve as the church.* This means identifying our spheres of influence, recognizing those sources of irritation, and yes, even paying attention to our career ambitions. Yes, the fingerprint of God could very well be on these things!

Likewise, the earth will not be filled with glory through some cosmic takeover (that is, until the Second Coming of

Christ); it will happen as both sons and daughters, men and women, *rule together* as Kingdom ambassadors at the gates of influence throughout the earth.

MARY: AN INVITATION TO PARTNER WITH YOUR PROMISE AND PROPHECY

Consider Mary, the mother of the Messiah. Mary is forever an exquisite case, because she was commissioned to "womb" the very Son of God. That makes her unique. And yet, we cannot lose her relatability in her uniqueness. Mary was a servant of the Lord, just as we are. She was a frightened teenaged girl who received a promise through supernatural means (the angel Gabriel). Revisit the story for a moment to grasp the context.

> *In the sixth month the angel Gabriel was sent from God to a city of Galilee named Nazareth, to a virgin betrothed to a man whose name was Joseph, of the house of David. And the virgin's name was Mary. And he came to her and said, "Greetings, O favored one, the Lord is with you!" But she was greatly troubled at the saying, and tried to discern what sort of greeting this might be. And the angel said to her, "Do not be afraid, Mary, for you have found favor with God. And behold, you will conceive in your womb and bear a son, and you shall call his name Jesus. He will be great and will be called the Son of the Most High. And the Lord God will give to him the throne of his father David, and he will reign over the house of Jacob forever, and of his kingdom there will be no end." And Mary said*

to the angel, "How will this be, since I am a virgin?" (Luke 1:26-34)

This promise would not manifest instantly, in the same way that your promise or prophecy has not come to pass instantly. And yet, I know for a fact that the promise Mary received did not join the ranks of the dusty volumes I saw in the library vision. Even though there was a process (roughly nine months) between her promise and manifestation, Mary made a decision to partner with what Gabriel said to her. Her mind tried to comprehend the assignment, as evidenced in her question to Gabriel: *How will this be?* Perhaps your prophetic word or promise or Kingdom assignment causes your mind some trouble. In fact, I pray that the daughters of God would receive more assignments that "trouble" their minds—not trouble as in bringing about pain, but trouble as in confronting the safe, comfortable lanes that society and even religion have tried to keep people in. When assignments, promises, and prophecies trouble our minds but make our spirits come alive, there is a high likelihood we are receiving a divine assignment.

What happened next with Mary? She talked with Gabriel about what was confusing her mind. Look at the exchange for a moment:

> *And the angel answered her, "The Holy Spirit will come upon you, and the power of the Most High will overshadow you; therefore the child to be born will be called holy—the Son of God. And behold, your relative Elizabeth in her old age has also conceived a son, and this is the sixth month*

*with her who was called barren. For nothing
will be impossible with God"* (Luke 1:35-37).

*And Mary said, "Behold, I am the servant of
the Lord; let it be to me according to your word."
And the angel departed from her* (Luke 1:38).

In spite of the ridicule she would face. In spite of all
the rejection and misunderstanding and loneliness that
would come against her. Yes, in spite of her own fiancé,
Joseph, not fully understanding what she was mixed up in,
Mary still said "Yes."

So often, when the assignments that God gives to us
are beyond our minds' ability to comfortably comprehend,
we "shelve" them. I prophesy over you right now, daughter of God, that the breath of the Holy Spirit is blowing
in this season upon those past prophecies and promises
you received. For those feeling frustrated and direction-
less, I actually believe that your "next steps" are contained
in some former words. The "word" you need in this season to set you on a course for breakthrough might be
written down, somewhere, on a piece of paper or in a
file somewhere. I believe the Spirit of God is summon-
ing you into the libraries of unfulfilled prophecies and
unanswered prayers!

WOMEN ARE A FULFILMENT TO AN
UNFULFILLED "END TIMES" PROPHECY

Perhaps the greatest unfulfilled prophecy is what we read
about in Acts 2. While there has been much debate and
discussion concerning the unfolding of specific end-times
events, there is a sure prophetic word straight from the

mouth of God Himself that unveils His will for the *last days*. Consider it here, as Peter preaches the first sermon following the Spirit's outpouring. In this moment, he is trying to give words and definition to the unusual manifestation of the Holy Spirit that was taking place.

> *But this is what was uttered through the prophet Joel: "And in the last days it shall be, God declares, that I will pour out my Spirit on all flesh, and your sons and your daughters shall prophesy"* (Acts 2:16-17).

Yes, this word has been partially fulfilled. We have seen a measure of Holy Spirit outpouring take place over the last two thousand years, and for this we are profoundly grateful. Yet, we have not seen God's target completely hit. Remember, His heart burns for *all flesh* to encounter the Spirit and receive the redemptive work of Jesus.

I believe *all flesh* are waiting for both the sons and daughters to occupy their spheres of influence, not only fulfilling the Joel 2 prophecy, but also stewarding the prophetic words they have received. Right now, I see the Holy Spirit releasing a grace upon you, daughter of God. Pause for a moment and receive what He is doing. You know that library of unfulfilled prophetic words? I see the wind of the Spirit blowing off the dust on those books. In fact, I see Him intentionally directing you to words you received—or even more uniquely, words you did not receive because you did not believe you, as a woman, were qualified to receive them, let alone pursue the realities they announced to you. I break off the lie of disqualification in Jesus' name and prophesy, *arise*! Step into what He is showing you. Be reminded of what He's spoken to you.

WALKING UNDER AN OPEN HEAVEN

You, daughter of God, have an open Heaven over you. If the Spirit of God dwells within you, you have been given unrestricted access to unlimited resources that flow *from* Heaven *to* earth *through* people. That's the process. Resources, power, strategies, and solutions for every ill of society exist in Heaven. From healing cancer to releasing wisdom for governmental policy, God is not sitting in Heaven scratching His head wondering what to do. He's not lacking creative strategy. The Lord has solutions that He wants to release *from* Heaven *to* earth. The question is, *in what form will these solutions, innovations, and strategies come?* Through what vehicle will His power, deliverance, and prophetic utterance flow forth? God's method is people—specifically, man and woman. Because remember, in the Garden man and woman were commissioned to rule *together*. God blessed *them*.

Daughter of God, you have something that the body of Christ needs. You have gifts, talents, and passions that must be released, *not* hidden.

PRAYERS AND DECREES

Father, open my eyes to talents, sources of gifting, and even career ambitions that I have. Holy Spirit, my desire is to see Jesus receive what the Father promised—nations. I want to see the earth filled with Your glory, Lord. Show me how to take my place in Your plans and purposes coming to pass in the earth. I say "Yes" to You, Lord. And as I say "Yes," I ask You, Father, take me on a journey. Show me things (callings, giftings, talents, passions) that might be locked up or lying dormant that You have entrusted to me because You want to see these things released in the earth. **Holy Spirit, take me into the hall of unfulfilled prophecies and promises.**

I encourage you to read through old journals, writings, recordings—wherever you have written down things that either the Lord has said to you personally, dreams you've had, or prophetic words you received in the past—and pray through them.

BENI JOHNSON

ONE OF MY FAVORITE STORIES IN THE BIBLE IS THE STORY of Jael killing a commander of the Canaanite army. Jael means mountain goat, and it is said that her family came from the rocks of Engedi, the spring of the wild goat or chamois. I've been to the Hills of Engedi. It is not for the faint of heart! Bedouin women were responsible for everything concerning their household. They lived in tents in the desert, and it is said that they knew how to make, pitch, and strike tent pins. This gal knew how to swing a maul and hit the pin to nail her tent down.

One of the traits of the Bedouin was hospitality. So, when the commander of the enemy army, Sisera, showed up running for his life at Jael's tent door she put on the charm and invited him into her tent. Judges 4:18 says that Jael went out to meet Sisera and said to him, "*Come, my lord, come right in. Don't be afraid*" (NIV). So he entered her tent, she covered him with a blanket, and gave him milk to drink. As the story goes, Jael waited until he was sleeping and got her maul and a tent pin and drove it into his temple. The Bible says that she drove it all the way through his temple to the ground and he died.

Some may think the story is disgusting, but look at it in a spiritual light. One commentator, Mary Hallet, says that Jael's treachery was forgotten in the light of her courage. Despite the graphic nature of this story, it speaks of the potential of one woman taking a stand. Deborah was the great prophetess at the time, and she played a significant role in the Israelites' victory, but it was Deborah who prophesied about Jael. In Judges 4:9, Deborah is quoted speaking to Barak, saying, "*Certainly I will go with you... but because of the course you are taking, the honor will not be yours, for the Lord will deliver Sisera into the hands of a woman*" (NIV). Against the expectation of the time, it was a woman who would end the war.

Growing up, my one desire was to marry, have children, and raise them for Jesus. I loved staying home and taking care of my family. Today, I see hundreds of women who daily step into that role of stewarding their families, and their dreams excite me. We live in a time when there is more freedom for women, and much more is coming. Around the world, women who have lived in bondage for decades are now experiencing slivers of hope. It is a wonderful sight.

Each woman has a place—a calling—and God is saying to each of us, "Baby girl, what's in your heart? How can I help you stand up and take your place? Can you see who you are?" We are a sisterhood for our Lord, and every woman has been created to leave her mark in history. Psalm 68:11 says, "*The Lord gives the command [to take Canaan]; the woman who proclaim the good news are the great host (army)*" (AMP). With the message of Jesus on our lips, women are empowered to be a force for the Kingdom. Jael—a housewife—did her part. Now, it's our turn.

Chapter Four

WOMEN ON THE FRONTLINES

Patricia King

IN 2014, I RECEIVED AN IMPACTING SPIRITUAL VISION regarding women arising into strategic, effective, and significant places of influence in the world for the glory of God. I saw large, powerful waves rising out of the ocean and washing up with force on the shores of nations, continents, and mountains. The waves then turned into a great company of women representing every generation and culture. They scaled the mountains of influence in culture, forming conquering beachheads for the holy advancement of the Kingdom of God. This army of women invaded nations and entire continents with His love, truth, wisdom, righteousness, and demonstrations of power.

I heard the Lord say clearly, *"It is time for 'My great company of women' to arise!"* (see Ps. 68:11). Immediately following that vision, the Lord directed me to Jake Hamilton's song, "The Anthem." I meditated on this song for months, and it had powerful prophetic impact on my heart as I identified with the Lord's specific passion to free women, releasing them into their calling and destiny. Every word of the song resonated in my spirit as I embraced it and applied it as a powerful prophetic word from the heart of God for women.

THE ANTHEM
by Jake Hamilton

I can hear the footsteps of my King.
I can hear His heartbeat beckoning.
In my darkness He has set me free,
Now I hear the Spirit calling me.

He's calling
Wake up, child
It's your turn to shine.
You were born for such a time as this.
I can hear a holy rumbling and I've
begun to preach another King.
Loosing chains and breaking down the walls.
I want to hear the Father when He calls.

He is calling
Wake up child

It is your turn to shine.
You were born for such a time as this.
This is the anthem of our generation;
Here we are God,
Shake our nation,
All we need is Your love.
You captivate me.
We are royalty.
We have destiny.
We have been set free.
We're gonna shake history.

As outlined in the beginning of this book, Genesis 1:27 reveals that God created man in His image and likeness, "*male and female created he them*" (KJV). Therefore "man" equals both male and female. Verse 28 further reveals God blessed *them* (male and female) with a command to be fruitful, multiply, replenish the earth, and to have dominion. His expectation was for both men and women to walk together representing His nature and authority in the earth. His original intent was that together they would advance His purposes.

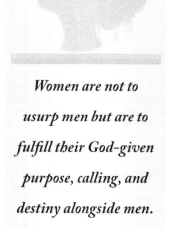

Women are not to usurp men but are to fulfill their God-given purpose, calling, and destiny alongside men.

Due to the fall, women have been a very oppressed people group, and it has not been until the last century that women's equality issues have even begun to be addressed.

This is an important issue to look at because until women come into their place beside men, we will not see the fullness of Kingdom fruitfulness or dominion in the earth. Although many western nations have experienced measures of breakthrough that produced some elements of equality for women, in most nations of the world women continue to be extremely oppressed and in many cases abused. Even western nations that have experienced measures of breakthrough have a ways to go in fulfilling God's mandate for women.

Women are not to usurp men but are to fulfill their God-given purpose, calling, and destiny alongside of men. Gender was not an issue when the initial blessing was released by God, and now in Christ there is no male nor female—we are one, together in Christ for His purposes (see Gal. 3:28).

DEBORAH: A "FRONTLINER"

One of my favorite women in the Bible is Deborah. She was a prophetess, judge, and wife. In Judges 4, we find her operating in her prophetic office as she delivered a prophetic word to Barak revealing that God would give the nation's enemy, Sisera, into his hands.

Barak was a powerful man, a military leader—the head of Israel's army. His name means "lightning," and he is found in the list of the heroes of faith in Hebrews 11. He respected the God-appointed office Deborah held as the prophet for the nation. As a result, he refused to go to the frontlines of battle without her. Barak was a seasoned and

God-fearing leader and knew the importance of having the Word of God with him to direct the battle.

In those days, only the prophets carried the word of the Lord. He needed Deborah on the frontlines with him to deliver the strategic word of God's direction in the midst of the battle. By following carefully the prophetic word of the Lord as she delivered it to him in the midst of the battle, Barak was assured of securing the promised victory. Together, each in their place, along with the armies of Israel and another powerful "woman on the frontlines" named Jael (who had a "tent peg anointing"), Sisera was conquered and the nation was freed from oppression. Following this nation-transforming victory, Deborah and Barak together wrote and sung the song of the Lord's intervention.

In the Bible and throughout church history we find many women appointed to the frontlines. Esther, Abigail, Mary of Magdala, Mary of Bethany, Joan of Arc, Mother Teresa, Maria Woodworth-Etter, and Aimee Semple McPherson, to name a few. God chose them, appointed them, and anointed them to fulfill His purposes. They were breakers for His glory and manifest power in the earth.

WHY WOMEN NEED TO BE ON THE FRONTLINES

Many might ask, "What are the frontlines?" The frontlines include any area where Kingdom invasion and advancement is needed. There has been much teaching on the seven mountains or spheres of influence in this generation revealing a clear invitation from the Lord to conquer enemy-infested and controlled territory. These mountains or cultural spheres of influence include religion, family, government, business, education, media, and arts and entertainment. Every one of these areas influence mankind's thinking, behavior, and actions, and as a result God wants His people to conquer, possess, and occupy these arenas with His truth and Presence.

There are many mandates in these arenas of influence that can be fulfilled by men or women (or both together) but there are definitely some areas where women would primarily be the ones appointed to break through a stronghold.

WOMEN ON THE FRONTLINES OF HUMAN TRAFFICKING AND SEXUAL EXPLOITATION

The Lord introduced me to sex trafficking when He directed me to take a scouting trip to Bangkok, Thailand many years ago. I remember the trauma of our first night on the streets as I observed so many young girls being bought for the night or weekend for sexual favors. Some of them looked as young as 14 or 15 years old, frightened and yet attempting to smile in the presence of their "clients." We soon discovered that children were also being exploited and that many of the children trafficked into Thailand were from Cambodia and lacked an advocate to speak on their behalf.

Both men and women on our team were full of compassion, desiring to make a difference, but the most effective on the ground at that time were the women. God has raised up powerful women worldwide to lead troops to invade this dark portal of human trafficking. We find men and women together embracing the call, but in some areas the women are more effective. Many of the young girls who have been trafficked have been abused by men and are not as open to them as they are to women. Women need to be on the frontlines of human trafficking and sexual exploitation.

Our first team into the refugee camps of Iraq, where thousands of Yisidi women were housed following their escape, was a team of younger generation women. Many of the women in the refugee camp, young and old, had been raped daily by Isis prior to their escape. Some of them were brutally raped more than 15 times a day. They were traumatized and frightened. You can understand why they might not initially be open to having a man reach out to them. Although there are wonderful men of God also on these frontlines, women are being powerfully used and called.

Light belongs in the darkness! Our light needs to be invasive on the frontlines of darkness.

Porn Conventions

Through the leadership of evangelist Cindy McGill, many women have engaged in extreme evangelism at porn conventions. I remember co-leading such an event with Cindy in Las Vegas one year where there were over 20,000 registrants attending from all over the world.

Pornography can have a dangerous effect on men, releasing an addictive chemical in the brain when they are exposed to it. Pornography does not normally have the same effect on women. As a result, it is much less vulnerable for women to serve on this specific "frontline."

It is an honor to represent the Lord in this dark arena—not to condemn those who engage in this life-damaging, life-destroying practice and addiction but rather to present Jesus to the afflicted through His love and grace.

A standard is being raised because of faithful women on the frontlines who are invading this arena with God's bold unconditional love and truth.

THE FRONTLINES OF GOVERNMENT AND JUSTICE

Many women are feeling called by God to the frontline of government service in this hour. Esther, in the midst of a critical and nation-destroying time in Israel's history, was courageously positioned on the frontlines and as a result brought deliverance to her people.

Faytene Grasseschi, is one example of a dynamic apostolic woman who is influencing government. She has raised up many of the younger generation in Canada to meet with hundreds of government officials in an attitude and posture of honor, submitting concerns to them. It has been very effective! Some of these young women are now running for office and some of them are currently working in Parliament in order to be on-site hidden intercessors and stealth servants of the Lord on this frontline.

Many women are arising in this hour to be a voice for issues of justice and with bold courage, love, and honor they are fearlessly bringing light into the darkness as they have influence on government levels.

Andrea Aasen, director of Everlasting Love Ministries in Cambodia, hosted a team led by Faytene Grasseschi into Phnom Pehnn who confronted the issue of abortion in that nation. At the time, there were abortion clinics on just about every corner. A pro-choice organization from the west had influenced Cambodians to abort their babies in order to help the problem of systemic poverty. As a result there were many women, even pastors' wives, who had aborted many babies without knowing what they were doing. It was discovered that some women had over 20 abortions.

This group of women on the frontlines educated pastors, doctors, social workers, educators, and government officials. Change began to take place as a result. Light belongs in the darkness! Our light needs to be invasive on the frontlines of darkness.

THE FRONTLINES OF MEDIA, ARTS, AND ENTERTAINMENT

God is calling many in this hour to the strategic frontline of arts and entertainment. This powerful portal of influence can affect culture for good or evil. If we abdicate our position on this frontline we are allowing darkness to prevail and rule over the hearts and minds of the current and future generations.

A number of years ago, the Lord called me for two years in a row to host an International Christian Film Festival in Phoenix, Arizona. At that time there were very few Christians influencing this realm through filmmaking. God instructed us to call forth submissions from all around the world and to celebrate each submission—no matter how polished or professional they were. We had a team of intercessors who prayed over each film and we aggressively prayed into this frontline inviting the Spirit to grant breakthrough. At the event we celebrated the emergence of God-fearing filmmakers.

Following those events, Faytene Grasseschi led TheCRY Hollywood, which was a focused intercession gathering of thousands in the heart of Hollywood. The fruit was amazing as we began to see a breakthrough of favor on faith-based and moral films. Some of the largest sales at the box office have been awarded to films that are clearly faith-based and containing a high bar on moral values. We have many friends in Hollywood who are pastors, leaders in the industry, talent, and passionate intercessors. Breakthroughs and beachheads are being established.

Miranda Nelson, a young Spirit-filled millennial revivalist, was called by the Lord to model professionally in Hollywood. In obedience to this invitation, she secured an agent and made herself available. As she filled out her profile she made it clear that she would not model lingerie and other garments that would compromise modesty. Her agent warned her that if she would not make herself available to model lingerie she would lose a lot of money. She responded to him and said, "That's fine; I'm not in this for the money." He looked shocked and asked her why she was modeling then. She responded, "I want to be an influence." He was very touched by her righteous passion and God gave her great favor that opened many doors and opportunities. On the frontline of the modeling industry she prayed for people's healing, shared the Gospel, and led people to Christ as she demonstrated the truth and purity of Christ through love. She was invading the darkness with light on this frontline. Many observed how she was favored in the industry even though she took an uncompromised stand. It was a powerful testimony to others in her field.

THE FRONTLINES OF HOME AND FAMILY

One of the most attacked spheres of influence today is the home and family. Marriages are being challenged, children are growing up without both parents, and in most homes both parents are working and therefore children often raise themselves.

God is calling women to be protectors of the home and family, and many are taking a strong stand on this frontline. One of our team members, Kylie Williams, is a mother of four young children, and her husband works in a career ministry position. She sees her frontline post for the Lord as being a minister in her home and to her family but has also reached out to her community through this powerful portal of influence.

Kylie is a ballerina, and her children love to dance. In order to nurture her children's dance passion, she launched XPressions Dance School and reached out to the community through this creative outlet. Young girls joined the school, and Kylie was able to influence them and their mothers with godly values, virtuous standards, and relationship. She then began a Mom's Connect group in her home where moms and their young children from the community came to her home and had "hang out time." She influenced them with her hospitality, love, friendship, and wisdom. She was transforming her community through her home and family.

THE FRONTLINES OF BUSINESS AND ENTREPRENEURSHIP

There was a day when women were not considered for positions in the business community, but the times have changed. Many women are being anointed as successful entrepreneurs and business leaders.

My good friend Teri Secrest was a single mom following a painful marriage failure. She was left to provide for her children. She did not want to work outside the home as her children needed her. Through prayer and seeking God for direction, the Lord led her to start a business that she could establish from her home. She worked hard and now, many years later, she has become a very successful businesswoman and is in the top 3 percent of women income earners in America. As a result of her success, God has opened many doors, and she has become an influencer.

The Bible introduces us to women who were successful businesspeople. Magdala was a business center, and it is believed that Mary Magdalene, following her conversion, became a successful businesswoman and, along with other successful businesswomen in her area, supported the ministry of Jesus. We also see women such as Lydia, a seller of purple (expensive) fabric.

God is raising up many successful Kingdom business-women on this frontline of Kingdom service who are not motivated by the love of money but who are filled with integrity and vision.

THE FRONTLINES OF EDUCATION

Women are becoming a strong voice on the mountain of education. This mountain of influence needs many more to labor on its frontlines. Children sit under the influence of educators all day as they receive input into their minds, hearts, and understanding. Many testify to losing their faith when they enter university programs and higher learning institutions. We need to arise and become an influence.

My friend Mary Printz created a learning accelera-tion program that has greatly influenced many—even those with learning disabilities, ADHD, and autism. Other women are homeschooling and reaching out to other moms and children with education alternatives and new curricu-lum that supports Kingdom and family values. Others are training to be teachers and entering the public school sys-tem in order to be an influence. A number are launching online institutions of learning. God is on the move!

THE FRONTLINES OF RELIGION

False religions are influencing the masses including west-ern nations that were established on Christian values. We are seeing a departure of many from church attendance and biblical beliefs. There is a clash of the kingdoms on this mountain of influence. More than ever before women are being raised up by God to herald His Gospel as evangelists, teachers, prophets, apostles, and pastors. They are coming alongside of men and making a difference.

One of my favorite women on the frontlines in our day is my friend Heidi Baker who is one of the most fruitful apostles in this hour making a difference worldwide as she advances the Kingdom by reaching the poor with the transforming Gospel of Jesus Christ. Prophets such as Cindy Jacobs and Stacey Campbell are also powerful influencers today. They are women on the frontlines breaking open new territory. I could write pages of names of women who are making a difference in the world today. In my Women in Ministry Network, women are serving in every area of ministry within the church and through the church and are successful and fruitful on their frontlines of service.

YOU?

What about you? Have you identified your frontline? This is an hour when God is calling for women to arise. He has need of you.

Wake up, child
It's your turn to shine
You were born
For such a time as this.

PRAYER POINTS

- Ask the Holy Spirit to reveal to you what sphere(s) of society He has called you to engage and transform.

- **Resurrection of career ambitions:** Pray for the Lord to reveal to you any career ambitions that you have put away in fear that they were not holy or sanctified. Ask the Holy Spirit to breathe upon these dreams and to resurrect the ones that He never told you to lay down. Religion might have told you to lay them down. Maybe even a church environment encouraged you to not pursue a certain career or direction. But the Lord never gave you confirmation to move in that direction. Pray specifically for *resurrection* for dreams that were forsaken and for *revelation* of God's Kingdom purposes through that career ambition.

- **Reformation in the frontlines:** Ask God to give you vision for what reformation *looks like* in the "frontline" area that you feel called and assigned to. Pray through this and perhaps journal it out, as it will most likely unfold as a process. But be specific in your pursuit. It's important to pray, seeking the heart and the vision of Heaven for what spheres of influence would look like in a transformed state, where those who walk in Kingdom values and are filled with the Holy Spirit are the people who are in high places of influence.

Chapter Five

WOMEN AND THE
NEXT MOVE OF GOD

*Holy Spirit outpouring will always be
partial when the voice and the presence
of the daughters of God are restrained.*

FROM THE BOOK OF GENESIS ONWARD, SATAN HAS BEEN on a mission to restrain woman from fulfilling her destiny as a co-heir and co-laborer with Christ. Yes, she is different and unique. Yet in Christ, she is qualified to rise up and boldly release the authority of Heaven on earth. It's only when this mandate is fully restored and its expression is *encouraged* in the church that we will begin to see Holy

Spirit outpouring demonstrated in a more complete and dynamic way. As long as woman is restrained from preaching and prophesying, biblically speaking, we are only going to experience a trickle of revival when God wills a river. This is because we are negating an entire gender.

I write from the vantage point of a man who is desperate to see the church operate in the fullness of the Holy Spirit. Responsively, I firmly believe that how we (men and church leaders alike) treat our sisters in Christ has everything to do with the measure of revival we *all* experience. This is absolutely biblical, for when Holy Spirit outpouring is biblically defined—both prophetically in Joel and then actually comes to fruition in Acts—women are specifically identified as those qualified to prophesy and participate in the move of God. The restorative work of Jesus truly leveled the playing field, making it possible for men and women alike to participate in releasing the power of Heaven on earth: "*There is neither Jew nor Gentile, neither slave nor free, nor is there male and female, for you are all one in Christ Jesus*" (Gal. 3:28, NIV).

As long as the devil is able to restrain women from taking their vital place in the body of Christ, he is likewise able to restrain a measure of revival and outpouring from flowing from the church and into the world. How is this even possible—and more importantly, is the concept scriptural?

WHAT IS CLOGGING UP THE RIVER OF REVIVAL?

There has been an age-old war raging between Satan and woman, the serpent and the Seed of the woman: "*I will*

put enmity between you and the woman, and between your
offspring and her offspring; he shall bruise your head, and you
shall bruise his heel" (Gen. 3:15).

Why are the efforts of hell so strategically targeted against women—specifically, trying to prevent women from occupying positions of leadership and authority? She is a unique and absolutely essential part of bringing the culture of Heaven to earth, unlocking the river of Holy Spirit outpouring that has been flowing since the Day of Pentecost. Make no mistake, the Holy Spirit has been moving since Pentecost; however, it seems as though His movement has been flowing with some hindrances, restrictions, and barriers during specific seasons in history.

The barriers are not on God's end; they are on man's. Jesus' blood sealed the deal and the day of Pentecost made God accessible to *whosoever will* receive the saving work of Jesus. In other words, God ensured that every barrier was removed so that you and I could be filled with His Spirit, walk in communion with Him, and release His Kingdom on earth. So why aren't we seeing this happen in a greater way? There are man-made barriers we need to confront. One of the most significant and unaddressed is how women can be marginalized in the body of Christ.

If the Spirit's outpouring was truly without restriction, then we would have no need for what we call "revival" or awakening; those seasons of unusual visitation become essential when the people of God engage in practices or entertain mindsets that build spiritual dams preventing the free flow of the Holy Spirit. He wants to move without restraint.

Sadly, one of the great dams and barriers to the Spirit's unrestricted flow in our world today is the restriction of women. When we restrict women from rising up and walking in the anointing to lead and prophesy, I believe we are—in part—restricting the Holy Spirit's movement on earth.

> *When we restrict women from rising up and walking in the anointing to lead and prophesy, I believe we are—in part—restricting the Holy Spirit's movement on earth.*

Before I continue further, if you are looking for solid scriptural support for why women should be in leadership, I encourage you to check out *Why Not Women* by Loren Cunningham and David Joel Hamilton, *Fashioned to Reign* by Kris Vallotton, or *Ten Lies the Church Tells Women* by J. Lee Grady.

BREAK THE RESTRAINTS TO REVIVAL

As long as the "daughters" are restrained from coming alongside the sons to *prophesy*, we will not experience the full measure of revival that God *wills* for the church to experience and the world desperately yearns to be transformed by. In fact, God more than wills it; He has already made it available! God has already said "Amen" to a landscape-shifting revival; however, the ears of God are bending close to earth, listening for those who say a whole-hearted "Yes" to everything He has made available. When men are the only ones who think they are qualified to say "Yes" to the call of God, revival is not being released in the full measure that Heaven has mandated.

When God spoke through the prophet Joel, He made Heaven's end-times agenda of outpouring and revival abundantly clear:

> *And it will be that, afterwards, I will pour out My Spirit on all flesh; then your sons and your **daughters** will prophesy, your old men will dream dreams, and your young men will see visions* (Joel 2:28, MEV).

If we didn't get the point in verse 28, the Lord emphasizes in verse 29:

> *Even on the menservants and **maidservants** in those days I will pour out My Spirit* (MEV).

As we know, the fulfillment to this prophetic announcement *began* in Acts 2 and has been continuing ever since. While there is undeniably an element of God's sovereignty involved in seasons of "revival," I have to ask: Could it be that one of the keys that positions the body of Christ for moving in sustained revival is the emergence of *prophesying* daughters? For centuries, the role of the "sons" has basically been assumed. There are really no questions or arguments over the leadership capabilities of men in a church context; however, a woman speaking, teaching, prophesying or leading is often the subject of considerable controversy. This shouldn't be!

WOMEN HAVE BIBLICALLY BEEN ON THE FRONTLINES OF GOD'S ACTIVITY ON EARTH

Throughout history, God's *daughters* and *maidservants* have been positioned on the frontlines of historic Holy Spirit outpouring. Sometimes they were dynamic public figures, pioneering revolutions and preaching the Gospel. Sometimes they were hidden in the prayer closet, literally contending for Heaven to invade earth through intercession. Either way, these women witnessed the fruit of their impassioned cries and dynamic efforts, be it during their lifetime or looking down from Heaven.

In the Old Testament, women are seen on the frontlines of battle, judging the nation, and providing refuge to the spies of Israel as they conquered Jericho. Women open and conclude the Gospels, ushering the Messiah into the earth and then beholding Him in resurrected form. Elizabeth gives birth to John the Baptist, the forerunner. You have others such as businesswoman Priscilla (see Acts 18:2-3), Junia (who many scholars recognize as an apostolic figure, see Rom. 16:7), and the virgin daughters of Philip the evangelist, who were *prophets* (see Acts 21:9). You have the Samaritan woman in John 4 who encounters Jesus, leaves her water pot, and preaches to the men of her city. As a result, they all experience a divine visitation from the Savior. Women are the first at the tomb to behold the resurrection miracle and receive instruction to share the good news with the apostles. And of course, there is the definitive woman of the Bible—Mary, the one whose womb delivered the Savior who delivered us from our sins, ensured that humanity could be indwelt by God, and ultimately birthed a revolution that would reconnect Heaven to earth.

It goes without saying that God has favored His daughters and has strategically set them on the frontlines of history. When God moved, it seemed like women were always there on the cutting edge of His activity. Elizabeth birthed a prophet. Mary birthed the Messiah. The Canaanite woman demonstrated a faith in Jesus that prematurely drew in a reality—the Kingdom of God being opened up to the Gentiles—that was reserved for the post-resurrection timeframe (see Matt. 15:28). These women all knew about collaborating with God and birthing Heaven on earth.

WOMEN HAVE HISTORICALLY BEEN ON THE FRONTLINES OF GOD'S ACTIVITY ON EARTH

Just review the pages of history. Revival after revival, movement after movement has seen prominent women serving as forerunners for what the Holy Spirit was saying and doing in that hour.

- **Maria Woodworth-Etter** introduced people to the Pentecostal experience before Pentecostalism became a formal movement within Christianity (in the 20th century). Her meetings were quite extraordinary. The Gospel of Jesus was always central, but the supernatural phenomena that occurred in that context were truly otherworldly. Healings, miracles, prophetic trances—

even those who came to mock these meetings experienced encounters with God.

- **Aimee Semple McPherson** was revolutionary in making the church experience relevant, interesting, and engaging, while also being a stalwart champion of God's miracle healing power. While McPherson was renowned for her engaging Gospel presentations, often drawing celebrities and Hollywood notables to her services at Angelus Temple, she did not back down from preaching the uncompromised Gospel—and preaching it in the power of signs and wonders.

- **Kathryn Kuhlman** could be best described as a friend of the Holy Spirit. She did not chase after healing miracles, nor did she ever claim to be some kind of faith healer or miracle worker. She rejected such descriptions. Kathryn was an evangelist, who passionately pleaded for people to meet her precious Jesus. She preached the Gospel with clarity, love, compassion, and gentleness—and healing broke out. Truly, Kathryn enjoyed such close fellowship with the Holy Spirit that when she walked onto a stage, audiences recognized that she was not alone; she was overshadowed by His Presence.

These are only three examples among the multitudes. I could go on and on about daughters who said "Yes" to God's call and have been changing the landscape of Christianity, both then and now.

Joyce Meyer is a no-nonsense Spirit-filled teacher and preacher, anointed to help make the Scriptures practical for everyday living. **Marilyn Hickey,** now in her 80s, is preaching the Gospel with boldness overseas (in some very difficult to reach areas), with mighty healing and miracles following her presentation. **Cindy Jacobs** is a prophetic and intercessory strategist who contends with Heaven for societal revival and reformation. When she prophesies, thunder breaks out. Australian worship leader **Darlene Zschech** was a key catalyst in the mid-1990s, used to release the sounds of Heaven into the earth and help pioneer the modern worship movement. **Karen Wheaton** is a contemporary apostle who has led a youth movement in the backwoods of Hamilton, Alabama for 20-plus years, raising up the next generation to usher in awakening. **Heidi Baker** has given her life to seeing the nation of Mozambique transformed by the love of Jesus—and in doing so, she and her husband founded Iris Ministries, which has seen over a million people come to Christ, churches planted across the earth, the sick healed, and even the dead raised. **Lisa Bevere** is a bold prophetic voice who awakens the roar of the Lion of Judah in the daughters of God.

The list continues and grows very long!

We honor the daughters in the earth who have paid the price for revival and reformation. **Beni Johnson, Carol Arnott, Brenda Kilpatrick,** and **Kathy Gray**—you have said a resounding, continuous, and costly "Yes" to the divine disruption of God called revival. And not only that, you have mentored the nations on how to steward the outpouring of the Holy Spirit. **Stacey Campbell,** your voice has prophesied the word of the Lord with fire and accuracy while leading a movement with your husband to release God's love, compassion, and justice into the darkness. **Joan Hunter,** you have not simply continued an amazing legacy; you have stepped into new dimensions of activation and impartation when it comes to training others to release Jesus' healing power. **Barbara Yoder,** you provoke us all to release the anointing that breaks things loose in the spirit realm. **Christine Caine,** your ministry is not only rescuing women from the unspeakable nightmares of the sex trafficking industry, your voice is breaking things open in the spirit realm and causes darkness to tremble. **Jane Hamon,** you have called a generation of Deborahs to arise and have taught them how to prophesy!

Surely, there are many names we are missing, and for those who are not listed, you, your voice, and your assignment are just as powerful and worthy to be honored as those mentioned. They are recognized by Heaven and the countless lives you continue to impact.

HOW WOMEN USHER IN REVIVAL

So as women, why does the enemy war against you and try to keep you from taking your place?

Here are *three ways that women uniquely usher in revival and crush the devil.* Make no mistake, the enemy doesn't want God's daughters to live mindful of these realities!

1. Women give birth to the impossible and remind Satan of his eternal defeat.

Mary was not some otherworldly super-being; she was an ordinary teenaged girl upon receiving her summons. Yet she deserves to be honored as a revivalist and powerful example of how anything is possible when one says "Yes" to Jesus. No one is beyond ushering in a great move of God! You were born to birth things into the earth—and in a way, you uniquely get to give birth to the expression of Jesus, because the Spirit of God lives within you and empowers you to manifest the nature, character, image, and power of the risen Christ through your life! Every time you demonstrate the work of Jesus through your life, you are enforcing the victory of the One who forever crushed the devil at Calvary. Women walking in this identity continually remind the enemy of his eternal defeat. When salvation is brought to a life or household, Satan is crushed. When healing reverses sickness, Satan is crushed. When immorality, crime, and corruption are exchanged for peace, honor, and love, Satan is defeated, yes—but he continues to be crushed as sons and daughters actually *walk* out this victory that Jesus purchased for them and enforce it.

2. Women sustain revival from generation to generation.

A woman must never devalue her ability to be a life-giver and life-bearer. You carry the ability to bring life into the world that perpetuates the move of God from generation to generation. This is the commission of every mother, natural and spiritual—to birth children who *sustain* and *excel your supernatural momentum.* The next generation should always be positioned to exceed the previous generation. If you have a womb, you have the ability to give birth to sons and daughters who prophesy, perform signs and wonders, heal the sick, lead movements, and change nations. You have the ability to raise up boys and girls, young men and young women who go further and deeper in God than you ever dreamed possible because God works generationally. Whether you have natural children or not, whether you can give birth or not, women are spiritual mothers who raise up a generation of men and women to birth the purposes of God into the earth.

3. *Women preach and shift atmospheres over entire cities.*

One evidence of the Acts 2 outpouring is that daughters will *prophesy*. To prophesy is to speak forth! You cannot prophesy silently. Need Bible references? The Samaritan woman at the well in John 4 went back to her town and "*told* the people there" about Jesus. And some of these people she *told* were men! As a result, the people left the town, went to see Jesus, begged Him to stay with them, experienced a two-day visitation from the Son of God, and many became believers. She preached and became a catalyst for a city to experience a divine visitation from Jesus Himself. How many more cities could experience powerful Holy Spirit visitation if women were encouraged to *go and tell?* Preach. Proclaim. Disciple. Prophesy. Jesus did not rebuke this woman for going; likewise, I do not believe He is rebuking His daughters today as they rise up, take their place, and begin saying what the Father is saying.

It's time for women to usher in the Holy Spirit outpouring they were anointed to release! From the Day of

Pentecost until now, the daughters have been qualified to prophesy. Let us encourage them to boldly speak forth the Word of the Lord, expecting their participation to release the fullness of God's Kingdom on earth!

BARBARA YODER

RECENTLY I NOTED THAT DOORS ARE OPENING FOR women in an unprecedented degree. This is the beginning fulfillment of God's prophetic word that this is exactly what He was going to do. At the time of this writing, the United States Secretary of State was removed by the President. This set a course of events into place. The CIA director replaced the Secretary of State. This opened up the way for the director's assistant to move into place as the CIA director. It just so happened that person was a woman and also the first woman ever to head the CIA. Hollywood is using more and more women producers for the film industry. Historically, it's been primarily a man's job. There are many other examples. History is in the making!

You and I as women are to awake! There is a fresh move among women to come into the place God has for them. In Judges 5, God said to Deborah, "Awake!" It reminds me of the passage in Ephesians 5:14 where it says *"Awake, you who sleep, arise from the dead"* (MEV). The Greek word for *awake* there is to open your eyes, see what is before you, see what God is doing in the spiritual realm, stop sleeping, and wake up, stand to your feet, get on the alert, watch, be vigilant, and to come out of obscurity.

Deborah had an epiphany! Her words were, *"I, Deborah, arose as a mother in Israel"* (Judg. 5:7). Today, a mother would be considered an apostle, a visionary, a general, a leader of an army, and therefore a leader into war. She not only awakened to the call, the mandate, but to the national crisis as well. When she awoke, she stood up, stopped her inactivity, and began to see things as they really were. She then stepped out of obscurity, out of the shadows into the limelight because she'd had an encounter with God. He called her to *awake!* She was already the leader but asleep on the job.

When a leader awakens, those following that leader wake up.

Because she woke up, she created a whole domino effect throughout Israel. When a leader awakens, those following that leader wake up. Something happens on a corporate level; an earthquake of shifts start rolling out. An awakening in the spiritual atmosphere we affect happens. We are more powerful than we think. When we wake up and take our place, a whole core of others following us awaken. And we call them to awake.

Deborah looked at Barak, saw him for who he was (who God designed him to be) because she awoke, and called him into place as the leader of the army. Together they marched into war to defeat Israel's enemy. A nation awakened and began to overthrow that which was out of order. In pursuing the enemy, the general fled and ended up in the tent of a housewife, Jael. Jael put him to sleep and pounded the nail through his skull, killing him. The enemy was defeated.

This is a new day when a massive shift is occurring in the gender realm. God is loosing women to awake and arise, moving into new dimensions of leadership. We are going to see the realms they lead shake society and shift this nation. This is the day that the Lord has made. We are going to rejoice even greater than ever when victory after victory begins rolling out because a woman awakened, crawled out of obscurity, stood up, and activated real and measurable change in the realm through deliberate focused action.

Chapter Six

ARISE AND ADVANCE, DAUGHTER PROPHETS!

HOLY SPIRIT OUTPOURING IS INCOMPLETE AND PARTIAL until the daughters of God take their place.

> *And in the last days it shall be, God declares, that I will pour out my Spirit on **all flesh**, and your sons and your **daughters** shall prophesy* (Acts 2:17).

All flesh. Not just sons and male servants. *Sons and daughters.* We don't have a complete manifestation of Holy Spirit outpouring without the visible emergence of God's daughter-prophets. This is the time for women of faith to arise, emerge, and boldly declare the Word of the Lord!

SUPERNATURAL INFLUENCE FOR THE DAUGHTERS

The Lord wants to entrust you with supernatural influence. He is going to use you to "influence the influential." Yours will be a voice with more influence than the actual influencer—because your voice, anointed by His voice, is what influences the one whose influence shapes movements.

These prophet-daughters are moms. Wives. Very normal people with normal lives. I see you cleaning spaghetti off your kids, taking care of your households, working jobs—the "everyday" things that are often considered mundane will be the very things the Lord uses to create an infrastructure in your life to steward the high level of influence He desires to entrust you with. Every time you clean a dirty diaper, you may not *feel* like a prophet to the nations, but the Lord would say that this level of service to your family is what sustains a humility and down-to-earthness that is essential in this hour. This *realness* will connect you with the next generation that craves your influence.

A WOMB WHO BIRTHS REVIVAL AND OUTPOURING

As we move closer to the conclusive move of God, the voice of the daughter-prophets will be essential *to the sons.*

The Lord is calling forth His women *out* of hiding in the women's conference circuit and into the church as a whole.

I see men holding women in greater levels of honor and respect than ever before, as there is something a woman can do that a man cannot—and even if he could do it, truly, I don't believe he would have the nerve or strength to go through with it. *Give birth.*

For the Lord would say, "I am calling forth My daughter-prophets in this hour to show the sons how to give birth in the Spirit."

One thing this generation knows *little* about is birthing in the spirit. Contending. Tarrying. Travailing. "Praying through."

We have a generation operating in the measure of the Spirit's power—healing, prophecy, power evangelism, etc. I celebrate this, but I refuse to put a ceiling on it and classify where we currently are as *the ultimate move of God.* I'm crying out for the Welsh Revival that transforms a country. I'm asking for an Azusa that births an unstoppable movement. I'm contending for a Great Awakening that revives the church and reforms the planet. I truly celebrate what we carry with the Holy Spirit and what we are presently seeing released—but I am also contending for more!

The daughter prophets will emerge in this hour with a word on *birthing revival* that breaks the ceiling of complacency in the church.

They will release burning words that send men to their knees, contending for the full inheritance of outpouring they have neglected due to lazy theology. I see the daughter prophets releasing words that birth the spirit of *tarrying* that ultimately ushers in the revival that never ends, where we fully pick up where Pentecost left off and step into greater realms of Kingdom increase and advancement.

CALLING FORTH THE YOUNG WOMEN—TEENS AND TWENTIES

I see the daughter-prophets in their 30s releasing words over young women in their teens and 20s that call them out of the world and summon them into their destinies and mantles.

The Lord says, "Religion's response to sin will not compel a generation to pursue Me passionately. 'Don't do this,' 'don't date him,' 'don't watch/listen to that,' is simply not enough. They need to have a vision—not of what they are being told to leave behind, but a clear view of the assignment they are being called into. I am calling My daughters to turn from sin *toward* their prophetic destiny to shape nations, release Kingdom innovation, operate in signs and wonders, receive creative strategies from Heaven, see into the spirit realm, dream dreams, experience visions and visitations, and take their place as My mouthpiece."

Prophet-daughters, your words will call forth a generation of Kathryn Kuhlmans, Marie Woodworth-Etters, and Aimee Semple McPhersons. In previous generations, these dynamic women were few and far between. But because of the assignment upon you, you will release a *vision* of what's possible for every woman filled with the Holy Spirit. You will release a vision to the next generation that will be superior to sin and more compelling than worldly compromise.

Daughter-prophets, you are called to share testimonies of these great women of God who were never meant to be the exception but the blueprint. You are meant to call forth the next generation of preachers, prophets and miracle-workers, doctors and lawyers, singers and songwriters, artists and dancers, innovators and entrepreneurs. What's the missing link? The next generation needs to hear that *it's possible.*

GENERATIONAL ALIGNMENT

The Lord is calling forth previous generations to come into alignment with this emerging generation: "You are not simply coming alongside young women to serve as champions and mentors—your assignment goes even further. When you come into alignment with what I am doing in the present generation, it's not just about My people, it's about My purpose."

Consider the prophetic pioneers of the faith, both the visible and hidden. Both have equal standing in Heaven. There are names you know, but there are also those you don't know who are equally as known in Heaven as the more famous ones.

All of these women forerunners did two key things— they prayed and prophesied. They prayed for a day when both the sons and daughters could fulfill their assignments in revival together, but their lives, their courage, and their boldness prophesied of what would be possible for all daughters of God to step into.

ARISE AND ADVANCE, DAUGHTER-PROPHETS!

Daughter-prophets—arise and advance! It's time for you to *arise*, embrace this calling and assignment, and it is time for you to advance. This means that you take everyday, little steps toward fulfilling this assignment.

Don't despise the un-glamorous steps along the journey, for the very generation that's waiting for you is *not* looking for glamour. They don't want a spiritual show. They want authenticity. They want real. They want diapers and disappointment. They want to hear about the breakthrough and breakdown. They want the pure, the real.

I prophesy, the very thing that will call forth an army of anointed, dynamic Kathryn Kuhlmans will be the 30-year-old mom-wife who shows, through her everyday life, that *any* woman willing to say an unqualified "Yes" to Jesus can steward a mantle that ushers in Holy Spirit outpouring and reforms nations.

Chapter Seven

God is Distributing Swords and Mantles to His Daughters

THIS IS A PROPHETIC WORD I RECEIVED CONCERNING THE daughters of God in this hour, and I want to share it with you just as I received it:

> *The Lord is handing out swords to women in this hour!* A sword represents authority. A sword qualifies you to fight. A sword is not a shield. A shield is defensive, but a sword is offensive.

In the spirit, I see the King of Glory knighting women with swords, as if to authorize them to offensively advance the Kingdom into spheres of society that demand solutions only Holy Spirit can provide. When men carry these solutions, half of the assignment is being accomplished—and that's great. But when the Spirit was poured out, men represented only half of the containers purposed to carry God's glory, power, and strategies into the earth; women are the missing link. I believe God's wonder *women* are the key to unlocking the fullness of outpouring into the earth, an outpouring that will only come to the world *through* the people of God.

The Lord is releasing women from the restraints of the "women's conference circuit." As daughters of God, you carry messages, anointings, talents, and leadership abilities that are purposed to bring solutions to problems. It's not just solutions for women; it's solutions for both the body of Christ and society at large.

For too long, Christianity has perpetuated a "women's conference" mentality, where anointed and gifted women "preachers" are given opportunities to share what Holy Spirit has put on their hearts—but in a restrained setting, women-to-women. Yes, continue to have women's conferences. Yes, continue to ensure that women disciple women. The problem is this cannot be all there is.

I prophesy that the hour is at hand when women are going to be released from exclusively speaking to women. Because they have been "knighted" by their Father in Heaven, I see the daughters of God arising to boldly declare the Word of the Lord to the church and release supernatural solutions into the broken parts of society.

The Lord is releasing mantles to women. A mantle was passed from Elijah the prophet to Elisha, his successor. In Charismatic circles, we have this picture of receiving someone else's mantle. *I want the mantle of Wigglesworth* or *I want the mantle of Kuhlman.* This cheapens what mantles are, as they are *not* for a human being to give, nor are they exclusive property of one person or another. Mantles are God's to give, and they represent supernatural power for specific assignments.

The Spirit is not passing out mantles based on the qualification of gender. Woman of God, if you read historical examples of men serving as catalysts for national awakening, for engaging cultural crisis, and for shifting the course of history, I sense the Holy Spirit is asking you a question: *Do you want it?* How do you know that God might have one to give you? Simple.

- What problems in society or the church particularly burden you? Do you have a passion to bring solutions to these issues?

- What stories and historical figures cause your heart to burn? Those past examples are testimonies of what measure of change and transformation is possible through an able and willing man or woman.

Mantles are not for a Charismatic showcase—to show off our power, gifts of the Spirit, abilities, etc. Mantles provide "ability" to your willingness (more about the willing part below). They are endowments of unusual supernatural power and strategy—not so you can appear spiritual, but so you can solve problems through the Holy Spirit's means and methods. Mantles are the exclusive property of God and God alone; He distributes them as He sovereignly desires. And yet, the Sovereign God is searching the earth for those who are filled with His Spirit, burdened for what burdens Him, and asking for a mantle of transformational power. So, what qualifies you to receive this?

What qualifies you for a mantle? While processing this word about mantles, I sensed that, for many women, there is often a wall. It makes sense for women to ask for mantles that were on the "wonders women" of the past—Aimee Semple McPherson or Kathryn Kuhlman or Maria Woodworth-Etter. But what about women asking for the mantles upon Billy Graham, Reinhard Bonnke, William Wilberforce, or Jonathan Edwards?

What makes mantles spiritually appealing are the end results we tend to focus on as recorded in history books—cities transformed, bodies healed, devils cast out, nations reformed, multitudes of souls brought into the Kingdom, supernatural strategies that release solutions, etc. But for history to truly and fully capture what's involved in stewarding a mantle—an assignment from Heaven with significant, measurable results—yes, end results must be presented, along with the *cost*. The demand. The price. And the question: *Do you want it?* How you answer this question determines your qualification to receive mantles from Heaven, regardless of the genders of the people who stewarded them in times past.

Do you want what those reformers and revivalists of old carried? Do you want that level of glory? Are you willing to pay that high of a price?

Gender does not qualify you to be used by God in a history-shaping, reformational manner. Gender does not qualify you to receive or not receive a mantle. Consider Paul's reminding words to the Galatians: *"There is neither Jew nor Greek, there is neither slave nor free, there is no male and female, for you are all one in Christ Jesus"* (Gal. 3:28).

What qualifies you is the same response that qualified every person throughout history who has ever been used by God—*will you say*

"Yes"? It's one thing to say "Yes" with your lips; will you say it with your life? Your "Yes" qualifies you for the mantle that God wants to give you, in the same manner that Elisha's "Yes" to Elijah qualified him to receive that "double portion" mantle.

A PROPHETIC RESTORATION OF THE GENESIS 1 DOMINION MANDATE

You were meant to rule and subdue *together*. Men and women, side by side, advancing the Kingdom in unity. The male is not less masculine because of the presence of a powerful woman. Likewise, the powerful woman is not hidden so the strength of the male can be given prominence.

When male and female—operating in their created capacities and identities—take up their weapons of warfare and fight together, I believe Satan will experience a nightmare scenario.

The redemptive work of Jesus on the cross set us free from the curse of the law (see Gal. 3:13). I often fear that the modern church is not aware of how expansive her redemption is. When the Spirit of God was poured out on Pentecost, power was released thus authorizing both men and women to advance the Kingdom of God on earth. The disciples asked about when the Kingdom would be restored to Israel, right? Jesus didn't ignore their question with His response; He just issued a superior answer. They were asking about some form of world takeover; Jesus introduced something infinitely more powerful and impacting.

Remember how Paul explained our Kingdom-advancing assignment: "*For though we walk in the flesh, we are not waging war according to the flesh. For the weapons of our warfare are not of the flesh but have divine power to destroy strongholds*" (2 Cor. 10:3-4). We do warfare in the invisible realm. As victories are secured in the spirit, there are measurable, tangible shifts in the visible realm. There are cultural changes. Governments are impacted. Bodies are healed. Torment is broken. This demands prayer and intercession, yes, but it also demands presence. It demands the Presence of God being carried by men and women into the epicenters of battle. Into media, arts, entertainment, politics, government, education, and every other sphere of society. It demands man and woman fighting together, without distraction. Without men compromising their distinctives and, likewise, without women laying down theirs. When men and women partner together to do warfare in the spirit realm, occupying high places of leadership and influence, a dominion is released that takes us right back to Genesis 1.

God's assignment to man and woman, together, was: "*And God blessed them. And God said to them, 'Be fruitful and multiply and fill the earth and subdue it, and have dominion over the fish of the sea and over the birds of the heavens and over every living thing that moves on the earth*" (Gen. 1:28).

God blessed *them* (not just him—Adam).

God said to *them* to "subdue" the earth and have "*dominion...over every living thing that moves on the earth.*"

When men and women fight together, lead together, preach together, and advance the Kingdom together, there will be a powerful manifestation of darkness being subdued and the "creeping" ones—Satan and his demons— being crushed under the feet of an authorized and anointed Ekklesia.

DECREES FOR YOUR ASSIGNMENT

I decree that you are receiving a sword in this season—a sword of authority for your assignment. I decree that, right now, you are being set free from any intimidation associated with the assignment the Lord is extending to you.

I break off word curses that have been pronounced over you.

I break off the lie that your words, voice, and your thoughts don't matter, either because they were rejected or because someone spoke over you.

I decree your words matter—if women don't prophesy, lead, and boldly speak forth, the fullness of Holy Spirit outpouring will not be released. It's a "sons and daughters" movement.

I decree that mantles are being released by the Sovereign God—not male or female mantles, but Holy Spirit mantles that release power for reformation assignments and callings.

I decree that you are qualified for these mantles, not because of your gender but because you said "Yes" to the One who distributes mantles.

For the Lord would ask: *Do you want it?* His invitation is not exclusive to a certain gender; it's simply for *whosoever will*. Take up the sword and step into your assignment. You are God's wonder(s) woman, anointed and authorized to release the wonders of His Kingdom into the earth!

Arise Reflection

HANNAH MARIE BRIM

As I was seeking the Lord in prayer about what to say to this generation, I was reminded of the girl Jesus raised from the dead: *"And he took the damsel by the hand, and said unto her, Talitha cumi; which is, being interpreted, Damsel, I say unto thee, arise"* (Mark 5:41, KJV).

I believe that He is also speaking to a future generation, saying, *"Arise,* and fulfill My great commission in all spheres of the world." I sense that there is a shifting that has occurred in the heavenly realm, and God is positioning His daughters in every arena of life.

God is calling us into a greater dimension of intimacy in the deepest places of His heart. He is clothing a generation with a robe of purity that the enemy has tried to strip away. The Holy Spirit is working in the hearts of women and overshadowing them into a place of holiness and intimacy where worldly desires melt in His love. I see the glory of God as a bright light shining through the faces of women throughout all the nations. I see a restoration of the mothers and daughters who have been separated, coming together to preach the Gospel.

I pray that as you continue to read the words in this book you will be ignited with the glory that is within you.

Father, may each daughter become so thirsty for intimacy with You. May they experience Your love for them in a deeper way and **arise** *into the place that You have called them to for such a time as this!*

Chapter Eight

A CALL TO
SUPERNATURAL
REVOLUTION

Patricia King

*These are keys and strategies that will
unlock the supernatural power of God
through any willing vessel, male or female.*

DURING THIS SPIRITUAL REVOLUTION, WE WILL SEE THE
restoration of the commission Jesus gave to His church.

Matthew 28:18-20 states: *"All authority has been given to Me in heaven and on earth. Go therefore and make disciples of all the nations, baptizing them in the name of the Father and the Son and the Holy Spirit, teaching them to observe all that I commanded you; and lo, I am with you always, even to the end of the age"* (NASB).

What were the things Jesus had commanded them that He was now commissioning them to teach to all the nations? In John 14:12, He emphatically declared to His disciples, *"Truly, truly, I say to you, he who believes in Me, the works that I do, he will do also; and greater works than these he will do; because I go to the Father"* (NASB). Jesus did many amazing works, but now He was decreeing that individuals who believe in Him will do the same works and even greater.

Oh how wonderful it would be if we did even a few of the works of Jesus. But if we are honest with ourselves regarding the current state of the Western church, we will have to admit that we are far from the model of Christ. Jesus performed mighty signs and wonders and operated in the supernatural. He encountered angels and the great cloud of witnesses, walked on water, traveled through walls, multiplied food, turned water to wine, healed the sick, raised the dead, cleansed the lepers, and cast out devils. This is the Kingdom of Heaven in action.

Whatever is real in Heaven should be real to us in the earth as we walk in the Kingdom realm. Jesus taught us to pray, *"Your kingdom come. Your will be done on earth as it is in heaven"* (Matt. 6:10, NASB). When we pray those words, do we actually believe them, or has the church been given over to lip service while our heart is far from Him?

As we embrace the spiritual revolution, we will be called to a restoration of Kingdom life, just like Jesus walked in. There is no sickness in Heaven; therefore, we should expect that it will not manifest in our midst, just as it didn't in the life of Jesus. Whenever sick folks asked Jesus for healing, He healed them. He walked in the reality of the Kingdom, and so can we. Jesus also came to destroy the works of the enemy; we have been commissioned to destroy those works as well. Are there demons in Heaven? Of course not. They were given the boot long ago, and yet we tolerate demonic assault in our lives. The revolutionaries who are being raised up in this hour know their authority in Christ and are committed to living it out by faith. Like Paul, they demonstrate the power; they don't just talk about it or preach about it. I want to be such a person.

In Matthew 10:1, Jesus brought His disciples together and gave them authority to cast out demonic spirits and heal every type of sickness and disease. In verses 7 and 8, He sent them off to preach the Kingdom of Heaven and commissioned them to heal the sick, raise the dead, cleanse the lepers, and cast out demons. This is what "preaching the Gospel" is to look like. They were to do the same works Jesus did—and they did! So can you, so can I. He said so.

I love the faith of many I have seen in the younger generation. They are radical and going for it!

Heidi Baker, a missionary in Mozambique, also impresses me with her faith. She shared a story with me of how she walked into a hospital where all the babies were sick and dying, having been infected with cholera during an epidemic. She held them in her arms in the midst of vomit and other diseased body excrements and loved them to health without ever contracting a disease, bacteria, or a virus. Her team often holds babies who have died in their arms and loves them to life. That's right, they raise the dead on a regular basis. This is normal Christianity.

Sitting in a church meeting for an hour or so a week, singing some songs, listening to a sermon, and giving some money in the collection plate is not real Christianity. This is not the fullness of the Kingdom. I don't want to suggest that those things are wrong in themselves, but true Kingdom life is much more than that. The spiritual revolution is challenging the way we do church. It is challenging the way we do life!

The following are a few reasons why the Western church is not moving in their God-commanded mandate.

Ignorance. They have not received teaching and therefore do not understand how to apply their faith to work the works of Jesus and flow in supernatural abilities.

Poor models. Where are the models of Kingdom life and spirituality in the Western church? Where are those who model the power of God as it is demonstrated in the Bible?

Fear of the supernatural. Most people fear things they don't understand. Because the Western church has been mainly academic in its orientation, there is discomfort regarding the things that our mind cannot initially understand. Spiritual things need to be spiritually discerned.

Wrong indoctrination. Some have received teaching that is contrary to the truth. For instance, in the

Pentecostal outpouring in the Azusa Street revival, many reacted against the revival by stating that tongues is of the devil and that believers were to have no part of this. In our day, many contrary doctrines to the Word of God are taught to believers. Things like prophecy is not for today, women cannot be ordained into ministry, believers cannot have supernatural or heavenly experiences, and only special people can minister healing or preach the Word.

Lack of results. Some have initially stepped out in faith to perform the works of Jesus, but because they haven't seen results they retreat to their comfort zones and neglect to press in.

Unworthiness. Many believers feel unworthy and as a result do not launch out.

Worldly-mindedness. The Western church is full of individuals who do not take their spirituality seriously. They attend church sometimes because it is the social thing to do, and they would rather go to a movie than spend time with the Lord.

Prayerlessness. Many in the Western church are a prayerless people. The disciples obeyed Jesus and tarried in the upper room until the power came. That happened to be ten full days of continuous and united prayer. Most of us do not spend that amount of time seeking God. In fact, many do not even seek Him more than a few minutes each day. A prayerless church is a powerless church.

Failing to do the Word. The Scripture says that if we only hear the Word and do not respond by doing it, then our faith is dead. The result—no fruit for our labor because there is no labor.

Sin. Disobedience to the will of God will always brass over the heavens. Sin is running rampant in much of the Western church, and as a result we are a powerless church.

Unbelief. Many will read the Bible and see the record of God's miracles, signs, and wonders but do not believe that it can happen today. Entire denominations have little or no faith in the supernatural operations of the Spirit. Where there is no faith, there is no entrance into the promised land. The Western church is plagued with unbelief.

Associations. If you hang out with those who are worldly or religiously minded and void of the Spirit, it could possibly rub off on you. You become like the company you keep. In Second Timothy 3:5, the Scripture makes a very strong statement and teaches us to actually avoid individuals who hold to a form of godliness but deny the power. That is a heavy word.

WHERE DO WE GO FROM HERE?

It is one thing to understand some reasons why we are a powerless church, but how can we actually get the power we need to live a real, supernatural Kingdom life? How can this type of life become normal to us? The following are some suggestions to help cultivate this true heavenly life in you.

Find some good teaching. There are many valuable seminars, conferences, books, and other resources available to the Body of Christ. Jesus said that you will know a good tree by its fruit. You need to check out various ministries to make sure that the fruit of the Spirit is operating in their lives and ministries and that they have a reputation for teaching the true and inspired Word of God. Our website at www.xpmedia.com has been created for this purpose. We feature many credible Christian prophets and ministers and offer a media site that is full of teaching on the supernatural, prophetic, signs, wonders, healing, deliverance, and prayer.

Reading biographies of those who work miracles and operate in the supernatural Kingdom realm is also very helpful.

Put the Word into practice. If you go to a prophetic seminar, then prophesy. I remember when I was taught to prophesy. After the seminar, I put the gift into practice big time! Before every prayer meeting, church gathering, and Bible study, I would pray and believe for the Lord to give me a word to encourage the people. At the meetings, I would step out in faith, most times with a bit of apprehension, but I went for it. The first year my words were very simple, but they became more specific and profound the more I practiced. You must "do" the word that you believe.

Associate with those who are walking in Kingdom power. Build friendships with those who have like passion and spiritual hunger. Sometimes, the Lord calls individuals to remain in a stale church environment in order to intercede, love, and bring influence to others in wisdom. If this is the case, then you must obey the leading of the Spirit. This is your mission field. I personally admire believers who obey the Spirit in these ways. Some, however, might need to plug in to another fellowship where they can grow. In other cases, the Lord might give an opportunity to get involved with an additional ministry that is sound and God-honoring while continuing to attend the local church fellowship. This could fill a void and help growth in the supernatural. We have known many believers who faithfully attend churches not open to the supernatural while at the same time building a relationship with our ministry team. This has been very helpful to them as they stay strongly committed to their call to their local assembly. Some Christians live in very remote and isolated areas and have no access to a Spirit-filled church that believes in the supernatural. This is a difficult situation, but with the web media today, good input can come from credible websites and resources. Some of our ministry partners live in isolated regions, but they often tell us how connected they feel to us as we build relationships through e-mail, prayer lines, letters, and the web resources.

Look for an outlet to minister the Gospel. Signs, wonders, and supernatural occurrences will follow the proclamation of the Word. God wants us to take His light into the darkness. Look for ways that you can reach the lost.

Fasting and prayer. As I have studied the lives of revivalists, healing ministers, and those who regularly operate in the supernatural dimension, I have noticed that most of them are given to extended periods of fasting and prayer. Jesus Himself, following a 40-day fast, worked many miracles in the power of the Spirit.

Invite the Holy Spirit to convict you of unconfessed sin that is blocking the pure flow of His power. It is important to note, however, that God's supernatural power is released and walked in by faith even when there is sin. I have known some ministers who moved in great power and supernatural acts, yet they had secret sin in their lives.

The gifts and the callings of God are without repentance, but make no mistake—whatever a man sows he will also reap. Eventually the things done in secret will be exposed and perhaps even shouted from the rooftops! If the Holy Spirit convicts you, then respond with repentance and receive forgiveness and cleansing.

Worship and soaking. Your fruitfulness will come from intimacy. John 15 teaches us to abide in the Lord. This is the greatest key to Kingdom life. Whatever you focus on, you will empower, so take time to focus each day on Jesus. He is so lovely. Soak in His Presence and allow His power to fill and transform you.

Aggressively choose to live in the supernatural. Oftentimes, we are very passive in our walk with the Lord. We might believe something to be true, yet we don't pursue it. We think, *Oh, maybe God might show up one day and zap me.* Although this could possibly happen, He is actually waiting for us to choose Kingdom life and walk in it. Throughout the Gospels, we see Jesus modeling the supernatural and then inviting His disciples to walk in it. The story of the loaves and fishes in Mark 6:33-44 is a good example. The multitudes with Jesus were hungry, and it was getting late. The disciples suggested that Jesus send them home, but Jesus said, "You give them something to eat." His disciples were shocked at what seemed an impossible task. It wasn't like there were any fast-food restaurants or grocery stores in the vicinity. Jesus then had them bring to Him what they had (a few loaves and some fish), prayed, and then gave them the pieces to distribute so that the disciples themselves would work the miracle. They were not supposed to be mere onlookers but active participators in the miraculous works of God. Look for opportunities to move in the supernatural.

WHAT IS THE SUPERNATURAL REVOLUTION GOING TO LOOK LIKE?

What will this glorious church look like in the midst of spiritual revolution? Perhaps it will look just like Jesus. Maybe we will see the church emptying hospitals, mental asylums, and even graveyards. Signs, wonders, and miracles will be normal in the time of revolution. God's people in the midst of the coming spiritual revolution will be practicing the things that we read about in the Scriptures. Kings and entire nations will come to the brightness of the rising of such a people. Hmm...sounds just like the revelation Isaiah had.

> *Arise, shine; for your light has come, and the glory of the Lord has risen upon you. For behold, darkness will cover the earth and deep darkness the peoples; but the Lord will rise upon you and His glory will appear upon you. Nations will come to your light, and kings to the brightness of your rising* (Isaiah 60:1-3, NASB).

Revolutionaries arise, for the spiritual revolution has begun!

Chapter Nine

DAUGHTERS OF THE KINGDOM REFORMATION

IMMEDIATELY, I THINK OF THE GROUP DAUGHTERS OF the American Revolution. How do you join this community? It is a "lineage-based membership" for women who are direct descendants of those who were involved in the United States' efforts for independence.

On the organization's website, it describes what makes you eligible to part of this community: "Any woman... who can prove lineal descent from a patriot of the American Revolution."[1]

Arise

As a joint-heir with Jesus Christ and a daughter of God, you have been grafted into a revolutionary lineage that is meant to release reformation in the earth. You all share the same ancestor—Jesus Christ, the Great Revolutionary.

I prophesy that the Lord is raising up a lineage-based membership of Daughters of the Reformation. Revolution will produce reformation. Often, the church undergoes seasons of revival, which are revolutionary. Everything we do is challenged. God comes down, reintroduces Himself in power, and our old ways of thinking, living, and doing Christianity are confronted—rocked to the core. Nothing is left unshaken. And yet, the earth has experienced revival after revival, outpouring after outpouring, and we have yet to witness sustained societal reformation. The revolution of revival must produce a people so transformed by God that they carry transformation into the very systems, trades, spheres, and assignments God has called them to.

> *As a joint-heir with Jesus Christ and a daughter of God, you have been grafted into a revolutionary lineage that is meant to release reformation in the earth.*

What God is doing right now through His women is absolutely revolutionary. However, it's not meant to simply be an awakening. An awakening ends with a restored

122

sense of personal identity. That's good and necessary, but it's a means to an end. Every Great Awakening is a means to an end—societal transformation.

You are awakening to who God has called you to be so that you can *be this person* in the place the Spirit has positioned you to transform. The very fact that the Spirit dwells within you is confirmation that you are anointed to bring transformation to *something*. Daughter of God, the Spirit within you will make injustice intolerable. He will make sickness and torment unacceptable. He will make darkness unbearable. When you're confronted with problems that demand otherworldly strategy, He'll speak. When you're in a position to bring solutions that release Kingdom order into your workplace, your trade, your vocation, your family—wherever you are—you can draw from the wisdom of the One living within you.

SALT, LIGHT, AND GLORY RISING

So why is God distributing swords and mantles to His women? He is equipping an army of reformers destined to release Kingdom transformation into every arena of society. Jesus wants us to be *salt and light*, correct? Perhaps we have become so familiar with the Savior's words that we have bypassed their massive meaning.

Daughter of God:

> *You are the salt of the earth, but if salt has lost its taste, how shall its saltiness be restored? It is no longer good for anything except to be thrown out and trampled under people's feet.*

You are the light of the world. A city set on a hill cannot be hidden. Nor do people light a lamp and put it under a basket, but on a stand, and it gives light to all in the house. In the same way, let your light shine before others, so that they may see your good works and give glory to your Father who is in heaven (Matthew 5:13-16).

Pause for a moment. Now consider the prophetic picture of Isaiah 60:1-3.

Arise, shine, for your light has come, and the glory of the Lord has risen upon you. For behold, darkness shall cover the earth, and thick darkness the peoples; but the Lord will arise upon you, and his glory will be seen upon you. And nations shall come to your light, and kings to the brightness of your rising (NASB).

For too long, we have embraced a theology of the end times where the church increases in glory, power, and impact *while* the world grows darker and darker, only to descend into absolute chaos and apocalyptic oblivion. Don't misunderstand me, I cannot ignore the influence and increase of darkness throughout the earth. I cannot embrace an end-times theology, either, that completely disregards the presence of darkness and evil. There is balance. So, what does this look like? I believe it's a combination of what Jesus says in Matthew 5 and the prophetic vision of Isaiah 60.

If the community of Spirit-filled believers, the church, is called to arise and shine God's glory, *what realm should be impacted by this radiating of light?* The world. The earth.

Culture, systems, and people who are under the influence of darkness. Let me further clarify. God's chief end is *not* to cover the church as the waters cover the sea (see Hab. 2:14), nor is it to pour out His Spirit on all *church people* (see Acts 2:17). His desire is to flood the *earth* with His glory and pour out His Spirit on *all flesh*. If Jesus said you are the *light of the world* and the *salt of the earth*, then clearly He envisions you—the light and salt—having some kind of measurable impact on the world around you. It's not "the church is going to get brighter and the world is going to get darker." While I understand this ideology, it completely disregards the words of Jesus that express how His people are meant to positively change the world around them.

Daughter of God, you are filled with the Holy Spirit. This is your identity. With this identity comes an assignment. As a carrier of the light of God's glory, you are qualified to invade realms of darkness. You are meant to bring the Presence of God into proximity to those disconnected from God. God has you where He has you because He wants *His* Presence there.

Every sphere of influence that Patricia listed in Chapter Four is open for your influence. As a woman filled with the Spirit living under the lordship of Jesus, your influence carries His influence. Your thoughts carry His thoughts. Your words release His words. Your mind is a birthplace for Holy Spirit inventions and innovations, solutions and strategies.

WHAT THE CHURCH IS NOT

To understand the move of God, it's vital to know what the church is *not*. The church is not a building. It's not made up of bricks and mortar or sand and stone. Of course, we meet in buildings, but just because we use a building as a meeting place does not mean that the building is the church; rather, it's the people who make up what Jesus introduced as the church in Matthew 16. The only thing is, Jesus didn't use the English word *church*; He used the word *Ekklesia*. He did not introduce a static location where people *came* and *attended*; He delivered a manifesto for an advancing, governing community of empowered people who were reformational agents in the spheres of influence they were assigned to. In these final chapters, Patricia and I want to present a prophetic picture of *why* the Lord is calling forth His daughters in this season, distributing mantles and swords. It all begins with the church—Ekkelsia—arising and emerging in its original, Jesus-defined expression.

> *Upon this rock I will build My church; and the gates of Hades will not overpower it. I will give you the keys of the kingdom of heaven; and whatever you bind on earth shall have been bound in heaven, and whatever you loose on earth shall have been loosed in heaven* (Matthew 16:18-19, NASB).

BINDING AND LOOSING

PROPHETIC WORD: WOMEN WHO LIVE IN TWO REALMS

I prophesy the Lord is raising up a company of Spirit-empowered women who live so near to Jesus, so close to the Master, that they operate in two realms at once. They live in Heaven, close to the Father, while also maintaining steady footing on planet earth. Steady footing—in that they are tuned into God while also wise in the ways of earthly culture. They must be in order to shift and change it. I prophesy that those who live tuned into the voice of the Lord both hear and see the culture of Heaven. As a result, daughter, you hear and see what is forbidden in the heavenly realm through your proximity to Jesus and your foundation in the Word of God. What's forbidden there must be forbidden here. No more, I declare! No more do you feel unqualified or unfit to boldly enforce the culture of Heaven here on earth. No more will the daughters of God shrink back, decreasing the volume of their voices. Raise your voice, increase the volume! Bind with authority, for there are spirits, principalities and powers; there are diseases, sicknesses, and injustices; there are forces of darkness that are running rampant, illegally, in the earth realm. For them to come to naught they must be commanded with a decree. They are commanded by those who hear His voice and, in turn, speak His word with authority. Daughter, you are equally authorized to rule on earth in Jesus' name and subdue the powers of darkness.

TheCALL visionary and prayer leader Lou Engle made a stunning statement concerning the assignment of women: "There are some spirits that only women can cast out." I believe this. When it comes to breaking agreement with demonic forces, we see multiple expressions of this phenomena being fleshed out in everyday life. As individuals, to experience freedom in Christ we need to repent from our sins and then break agreement with demonic lies, covenants, or activities that we have entertained. This process should be practiced by individuals, cities, nations, and, I believe, genders. Men and women need to ask the Spirit of God for discernment concerning what spirits have specifically been targeting their communities. We want to target these spirits so we can identify them and cast them out.

Woman of God, it's your time to arise and claim your place of spiritual jurisdiction. No, you do not have the

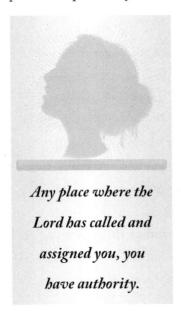

Any place where the Lord has called and assigned you, you have authority.

right to call out every principality, power, and territorial spirit throughout the nations, for you do not have jurisdiction in all places and among all people. Same goes for the men of God. Believers get into trouble with spiritual warfare when they take on powers of darkness that God did not assign them to combat or challenge. And yet, there are forces of darkness at work in the areas

of jurisdiction the Lord has uniquely given you—your life, your family, your job, your school, your city, and your region. Any place where the Lord has called and assigned you, you have authority. Be sensitive and aware of this. One way you can be sure you have jurisdiction in a certain area to bind hell and loose Heaven is by seeking the Holy Spirit and asking Him for a word of clarity. If there is an assignment that you burn to take on, present it to the Lord and seek Him. Consult Him. Spend time with Him. Talk to Him about what moves you. Saddens you. Inspires you. Compels you. Agitates you. I prophesy that in those conversations, the speaking God will speak to you. When God gives you an assignment, there is the surety of victory on that assignment because it comes from Him.

His assignments begin with His voice. He will speak to you and give you a word. Don't limit the ways He does this. It could be through a scripture, a prophetic word, a vision, a dream, unusual circumstance, etc. Either way, I sense that reformational assignments for God's daughters in this season will be birthed in the fire of Holy Spirit *encounter*. His voice speaks from the fire of encounter.

THE JOURNEY OF REFORMATION

Not only do we need to bind the powers of darkness, but we need to loose and release the Kingdom of God. I believe this "loosing" of the Kingdom will take place as everyday women have extraordinary Holy Spirit encounters, as these encounters will lead to reformational assignments.

We need Holy Spirit encounters.

The church was not birthed by ivory tower theologians but through everyday people, men and women, who were the recipients of transformational encounters with the Holy Spirit. In this hour, the church community must prize God-encounters. We cannot tolerate them at best, reject them at worst. We cannot allow our nervousness about what happens when people experience God to improperly motivate us to sterilize spiritual atmospheres in our meetings. I believe that daughters of reformation will be birthed in the fire of Holy Spirit encounter and outpouring. As the church continues to open the atmosphere to the move of God, allowing for His unusual touch to grace His people, I foresee the emergence of a reformation generation. They will have touched, tasted, experienced, and felt the reality and raw force of God in the place of encounter. As a result, they will return to their spheres of influence convinced that the God *inside of them* is the same as the God who *touched them* and that this God *in them* wants to change the world *around them*.

We need to steward Holy Spirit encounters by listening for the voice.

It's great to have a Holy Spirit encounter where we get powerfully touched by the Presence of God. I prize these in my life and in the people I am privileged to minister to. The problem is *what happens next*. This has been a great stumbling block to many people concerning the move of the Holy Spirit, as we are quick to identify the people who seemingly get radically touched by God, have a life-altering experience, and get up and go on with life the same as before or, sadly, even worse than before. We disqualify the need for encounters with God because we see a bunch of lousy fruit in people who looked like they got deeply touched by the Spirit. Here's the deal—bad fruit is not God's fault. Bad fruit happens when we don't *steward* the touch of God upon our lives. Too many people enjoy a Holy Spirit encounter, but they stop short of hearing the reformational voice that speaks *out of the fire of encounter.*

HEARING THE VOICE THAT SPEAKS FROM THE FIRE

In the Old Testament, I believe the "tent of meeting" is a picture for what we are, today, as a people filled with the Spirit of God. We are portable containers/tabernacles of the Presence of the Holy Spirit—this makes us walking, talking "tents of meeting." We can meet with God wherever we go; and likewise, we can literally carry meetings with God, encounters with God, into places, communities, and environments where people don't even know the Lord yet. You know what was unique about the tent of meeting in the Old Testament? It was a place of encounter and exchange. No doubt Moses enjoyed rich fellowship with the Presence of God in this tent. However, proximity to divine Presence was not the end-all; there was a voice that spoke out of that place of encounter.

We see this in the *tent of meeting* that the Lord instructed Moses to establish.

> *The Lord called Moses and spoke to him from the tent of meeting* (Leviticus 1:1).

People *sought and inquired of the Lord* at the tent of meeting.

> *Now Moses used to take a tent and pitch it outside the camp some distance away, calling it*

the "tent of meeting." Anyone inquiring of the Lord would go to the tent of meeting outside the camp (Exodus 33:7, NIV).

This is the place where God spoke to Moses.

When Moses entered the tent, the pillar of cloud would descend and stand at the entrance of the tent, and the Lord would speak with Moses (Exodus 33:9).

The first "tent of meeting" between Moses and God was not a tent or tabernacle; it was on a mountain and involved a bush, fire, a voice, and an assignment to liberate a nation.

Now Moses was keeping the flock of his father-in-law, Jethro, the priest of Midian, and he led his flock to the west side of the wilderness and came to Horeb, the mountain of God. And the angel of the Lord appeared to him in a flame of fire out of the midst of a bush. He looked, and behold, the bush was burning, yet it was not consumed. And Moses said, "I will turn aside to see this great sight, why the bush is not burned." When the Lord saw that he turned aside to see, God called to him out of the bush, "Moses, Moses!" And he said, "Here I am." Then he said, "Do not come near; take your sandals off your feet, for the place on which you are standing is holy ground." And he said, "I am the God of your father, the God of Abraham, the God of Isaac, and the God *of Jacob." And Moses hid his face, for he was afraid to look at God* (Exodus 3:1-6).

That first encounter at the burning bush is a prophetic illustration for what the Holy Spirit is calling the daughters of God into, both today and throughout all generations. Of course, the *sons* are called to enjoy these encounters too. But this has been a spiritual "given" for too long in the body of Christ. We expect men to have life-altering, history-shaping experiences in the Presence of God that launch them into ministries, careers, and reformational assignments. Now, it's time for the daughters to realize that they too get to share in the fruit of Holy Spirit encounter.

I prophesy, daughter of God, that your ears are inclined to hear the voice of reformation that speaks out of the fire. Many women have encounters with the Holy Spirit. That's not the issue up for discussion. However, I am convinced the daughters often don't position their ears to *hear* the voice of reformation that speaks from the fire because of a collective lie that has been propagated for far too long. It makes sense for Billy Graham, Reinhard Bonnke or Martin Luther. It makes sense for Wesley, Finney, and Edwards. It makes sense for the entrepreneurs, scientists, inventors, Noble Prize winners, Hollywood producers, and politicians...who are men.

The voice that speaks out of the fire is not directed toward your gender—it's looking for a response of surrender. The voice seeks the one—man, woman, child—who will *turn aside* and move toward the fire.

Then the Lord said, "I have surely seen the afflic-
tion of my people who are in Egypt and have
heard their cry because of their taskmasters. I
know their sufferings, and I have come down to
deliver them out of the hand of the Egyptians
and to bring them up out of that land to a good
and broad land, a land flowing with milk and
honey, to the place of the Canaanites, the Hittites,
the Amorites, the Perizzites, the Hivites, and the
Jebusites. And now, behold, the cry of the people
of Israel has come to me, and I have also seen
the oppression with which the Egyptians oppress
them. Come, I will send you to Pharaoh that you
may bring my people, the children of Israel, out
of Egypt" (Exodus 3:7-10).

What will this voice say to you? Many focus on the dramatic encounter that Moses had and the unique manifestation that occurred—the voice of the Lord speaking through a burning bush (and yet, the bush was not consumed). It's easy to miss a message by focusing too much on the manifestations.

As mentioned earlier, Holy Spirit power-encounters are not optional. Yes, we need to focus on making sure that the body of Christ is filled with men and women who know their reformational assignments and *act* upon them. Absolutely. However, assignments are distributed in the fire of encounter. At the same time, we cannot get so lost in the dramatics of the encounter that we miss the point.

Moses didn't just have a powerful encounter with God. Moses didn't just hear the voice of the Lord speaking out of a burning bush. Moses received an assignment—a reformational assignment. The same God who spoke to Moses is speaking today. He is speaking to you, and I believe He is ready to distribute mantles to His daughters. These are assignments that come with power and the assurance of victory.

As the Lord spoke with Moses, so He is speaking today. He has seen the affliction plaguing the earth. He has heard the cry of desperate humanity. His ears are in tune with the groaning of creation that evidences the bondage, addiction, torment, and suffering taking place upon its soil, among its inhabitants. He's not distant or detached. As revealed in Exodus 3, the Lord God *knows* their sufferings.

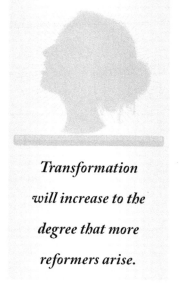

Transformation will increase to the degree that more reformers arise.

What's His solution? His announcement to Moses concerning the people of Israel is relevant to all times and all generations: "*I have come down to deliver them out of the hand of the Egyptians and to bring them up out of that land to a good and broad land, a land flowing with milk and honey, to the place of the Canaanites, the Hittites, the Amorites, the Perizzites, the Hivites, and the Jebusites*" (Exod. 3:8).

God is not somewhere out there in outer space, disconnected from what's taking place on the planet. Far from it. I prophesy that transformation will increase to the degree that more reformers arise. More reformers will arise as more women are told, "You too can be a reformer! You too can be a Moses! You too can be a Joshua!" It's easy for women to look at other women in the Bible—Esther, Deborah, Ruth, etc.—and see those heroines as examples to follow. That's true. At the same time, the Lord can use *you* as He did Moses, Joshua, Joseph, or Daniel.

DECLARATIONS OF DELIVERANCE

I break off restrictions that prevent you from hearing the voice from the fire. Specifically, I break off the lie that your gender disqualifies you—especially from fulfilling assignments that you have only seen, read, or heard about men operating in. Gender does not qualify you; saying "Yes" to the voice is what qualifies you.

I break off religious restrictions, in Jesus' name. The spirit of religion tries to turn down the volume of His voice, as the Spirit wants to speak specifically about assignments *outside of the church or religion mountain.* For too long, Christians have mistakenly assumed that the zenith of their service to God is expressed by serving in the church; no, it's serving *as the church* in the world. *Salt* in the earth and *light* of the world. In culture. In society. In the places that, sadly, the spirit of religion tries to prevent the church from intentionally reaching, these are the spheres in which God is calling you, His wonder woman, to have impact and influence.

He's calling you to the arenas of business, medicine, and law. He's anointing you for politics, government, media, and entertainment. He's giving you wisdom and strategy and creativity from the heavenly realm so that you can have the Kingdom edge. Why is it important that the women of God (alongside the men of God) ascend to key places of influence and authority in the different spheres of society? So that people who are filled with the Spirit of God can release the wisdom that comes from Heaven *into* the problem areas in these arenas. It's not about a takeover; it's about having Kingdom influence in the unseen realm, so that the life-giving ways of Jesus are revealed in the earth. As Kingdom solutions are released, they carry the Presence of the Holy Spirit upon them because of their point of origin. They originate, not from you, but from the One who dwells within you.

DECREES

I am filled with the Spirit of God. He releases supernatural power, wisdom, and creativity.

The Spirit of God within me gives me the ability to access Kingdom solutions to the problems, crises, and chaos I face every day.

I decree that because of the Spirit of God within me, I have access to the wisdom of another age. I can enter whatever situation I'm in, confident that if I ask Him for wisdom He will be faithful to provide it.

Lord, I am not asking for just an awakening. Awaken me to who You say I am and what You say I can do so I can be empowered to go out and do it. Lord, I ask for awakening. I ask for revival. I ask for Your Holy Spirit to move with unusual power. Let it be so in my life! Even now, I raise my hand and say, "God, choose me! I'm available!" I won't let it

Arise

end with me—I'll carry this revelation of identity and assignment into the places You have called me.

NOTE

1. https://www.dar.org/national-society/about-dar/who -we -are/who-we-are, accessed January 28, 2018.

Arise Reflection

STACEY CAMPBELL

*I will tell of the decree: The Lord said
to me, "You are my Son; today I have
begotten you. Ask of me, and I will
make the nations your heritage, and the
ends of the earth your possession."*
—Psalm 2:7-8

I AM SEEING AN INCREASING NUMBER OF WOMEN ASKING
God to allow them to influence nations of the earth! I
have worked with women to whom God has given strategies for reforming national economies, with others who are
running for Prime Minister, with others who are gathering

top leaders in multiple spheres of influence together to collaborate in eradicating corruption. Still other women are tackling systemic poverty as God gives them revelation on how to change the world, one poor person at a time.

Personally, I began to ask God for nations years ago. The strategy He gave me was to start with prayer because the house of prayer is for all nations (see Mark 11:17). We began first with a day of prayer, gathering regional leaders in the spirit of Joel 2. We gathered people to pray in government buildings, on mountaintops, in the heart of the city—thousands and ten thousands came to repent for the sins of the nation (like Daniel 9). The next step was to begin to catalyze houses of prayer around the nation by bringing in prayer leaders to teach and model building houses of prayer. When we started in Brazil, there was only one 24/7 house of prayer that we knew of. Now there are almost 300 houses of prayer in that nation. Finally, after years of doing this, when there was critical mass—enough prayer filling the atmosphere—we called believers in high level arenas together to create a collaborative model of societal transformation. And now the sound of transformation is being heard around the nation. We will not stop until we see nations shift!

Chapter Ten

Anointed to Occupy the High Places

When Jesus introduced the church in Matthew 16, He envisioned a radical community of people that hell could *not* prevail against. If the powers of darkness seem to be prevailing against the church, we need to pause and honestly ask ourselves the following question: *Are we operating as the church that Jesus defined, or are we just "doing church" based on some popularized model or method?*

HOW TO BE THE PEOPLE HELL CAN'T DEFEAT

I firmly believe darkness can prevail against a building, against an institution, against a business, and against a spiritual organization. I believe darkness can prevail against charity, social justice, and non-profit organizations. However, darkness cannot advance against the Ekklesia of God—the Holy Spirit filled community that has been anointed and charged to bind the powers of darkness and loose the influence of the Kingdom. That's why all of our efforts—social justice, charity, mission movements, buildings, organizations, programs—must be infused with a vision to be an *Ekklesia*. And what is the end goal of the Ekklesia? *Shaping culture.*

It is foolish of us to evaluate the success of the church based on how well a Sunday service goes, or how many people we have signed up for a certain program, or what level of engagement we have in our small groups. All of this is good, but cannot be the litmus test for the overall effectiveness of the church. How do we truly evaluate the fruitfulness and impact of the local church? We examine local culture. We evaluate local business. We consider local law and government. We intentionally look for evidence of the presence of the church in our communities, regions, and cities. The evidence is not a building. Many cities have multiple church buildings. Some places seem to have churches on every corner. And yet there doesn't seem to be evidence of an Ekklesia in operation. The evidence is not even a food drive or a community outreach once a week, month, etc. The true evidence of the church's impact is the everyday places where the people of God are positioned. From schools to business to government, how do these spheres of influence look *different* because of the presence of anointed men and women?

For too long, we've assumed the sons of God have exclusively been summoned to these tasks. But remember, the outpouring of the Spirit is not just for the sons—it's for sons and daughters, menservants and maidservants. Also, the outpouring of the Spirit is not reserved for the church; it's for *all flesh*. You have been filled with God's Presence and positioned where you are because God wants *His Presence in that place*. Furthermore, He wants you to have vision to ascend to the high places in that sphere of influence so His Presence can occupy the high places.

THE HIGH CALL TO THE HIGH PLACES

I believe one of the most un-accessed assignments of the modern church is occupying the *high places* for the Kingdom. Many are afraid of the high places because these are where the *gates of Hades* or *gates of hell* are located.

High Places of Government and Law

When hell controls these gates, immorality is legislated and viewed as acceptable practice. When the Ekklesia controls these gates, immortality is legislated against, not out of intolerance or lack of love for people, but to prevent darkness from having further destructive inroads in our communities. The Ekklesia legislates with radical love and acceptance for people while maintaining an uncompromised stance against sin. I prophesy that the righteous will begin to arise and rule in the high places of government and law, not with some agenda to overthrow and take over; they will be compelled by the heart of Jesus to love and serve people through Kingdom values. Let the righteous

rule and *increase* in these high places so the people of the
land *rejoice* (see Prov. 29:2).

High Places of Entertainment

When hell controls these gates, sin is presented as
fun, comical, and acceptable—it's presented through
movies, TV, music, and all formats of modern "art" as normal. When the Ekklesia controls these gates, art unveils
the glory of God, beauty of creation, severity of sin, and
message of redemption. The Ekklesia is arising in Hollywood, Broadway, and all "high places" of entertainment to
exercise dominion over the spiritual airways. Those called
to be missionaries in these places will be graced with an
anointing for prophetic intercession. Yes, these are terri-
tories under the influence of deep darkness; at the same
time, those legitimately called to be light in the darkness
will aim prayers over the spiritual airways controlling the
narratives coming out of the high places of entertainment
and, in turn, prophesy the purposes of God. The prophetic
intercession of God's media missionaries will clear the airways and create an atmosphere where even those who are
disconnected from God will receive inspiration and create
art that, ultimately, releases Kingdom values. Why? They
are creating under the influence of the dominion force in
that high place. You were created to occupy the high places
so you can shape the narrative that artists create out of!

High Places of Business and Finance

When hell controls these gates, wealth is funneled into
the purposes of darkness. There is no sacred responsibility
for how wealth is made or where finances are sent. When
the Ekklesia controls these gates, wealth is created by men

and women receiving prophetic blueprints from Heaven. Wealth becomes a solution that aims against the problems and ills of society. Wealth is not the final aim of wealth creation, nor is simply cutting a "tithe" or "offering" check. The ultimate agenda and assignment of Kingdom wealth creation is to aim finances at problems and release break-through solutions that usher people, systems and cultures out of darkness and into light.

High Places of Education

When hell controls these gates, a generation is taught that a God-consciousness is archaic. More than foster a debate between creation and evolution, absolute truth and relativism, the powers of darkness want to educate a gen-eration out of their created identity. If there's no creation, there is no Creator, and if there is no Creator, then there is ultimately no purpose. When the Ekklesia influences these gates, Kingdom representatives occupying positions in both private and public education systems communicate a message of purpose and identity. Even though there is much censorship in education concerning God, Creation, and the Gospel, Kingdom educators and administrators receive supernatural strategy from the Holy Spirit on how to communicate these truths and create *greenhouses of pur-pose, love, and identity* in their classrooms and schools.

ASK GOD FOR YOUR "HIGH PLACE" ASSIGNMENT

Ask the Lord for what high place you have been called and assigned to. I realize this language might be a little intimidating at first, as religious thinking has taught us that aspiring for greatness is contrary to the humble model of Jesus.

The truth is, no human being dreams of insignificance. In his transformational book *The Good and Beautiful Life,* spiritual formation author James Bryan Smith notes that "no one seeks a full, lifeless, boring, meaningless life."[1] Children have to be taught that insignificance is the path they are to pursue or expect. Otherwise, by default it seems like our kids have a built-in drive toward being superheroes, princesses, warriors, and astronauts.

The only reason we settle for insignificant lives is we have somehow believed that significance and influence are worldly. They are worldly only when they are divorced from radical love for and obedience to Jesus. When completely surrendered to Jesus, things like drive for significance, vision for greatness, and career ambition compel us to identify the spheres of influence we feel called to and then plant ourselves in these places with intention to ascend to the "high places." And remember, a "high place" is not necessarily the number-one Hollywood producer, or the President of the United States, or a Supreme Court justice, or a Nobel Peace Prize winner, or something to that effect.

A high place, in my view, is a sphere of influence that is under someone's authority. As a result of this authority, atmosphere and culture are created, representing the value system of the one who is in authority. You may have authority over a division. You may be a manager. You may be an administrator. You could have a business with employees. You may have a classroom. You may lead a club or organization on campus. I believe, daughter of God, the

Holy Spirit is calling you to the high places of your sphere of influence. He's calling you there because He wants you to have authority. He wants you to have authority, not to make a name for yourself. Let promotion come from the Lord. He wants you in places of authority because He wants those who carry His Presence to be the ones shaping culture and establishing atmosphere. And do you know why?

When the righteous—those filled with the Holy Spirit—have influence over shaping a culture or atmosphere, the environment becomes supernaturally charged. It becomes *easy* for people to have encounters with God and ultimately receive Jesus Christ as Lord and Savior. For those who get concerned about the alleged absence of the "Gospel of Salvation" in a message like this, I believe the desire of God to have His people in the high places is motivated by a powerful vision for evange-

The only reason we settle for insignificant lives is we have somehow believed that significance and influence are worldly. They are worldly only when they are divorced from radical love for and obedience to Jesus.

lism. He wants to see atmospheres created that are placed under the influence of men and women who are filled with His Presence. Remember who the great Evangelist is—the Holy Spirit. If a committed believer has jurisdiction in a high place, the Holy Spirit likewise has jurisdiction in that place. The key word is *committed*.

This message will only work and produce fruit for those who have a vision to see the high places influenced by King Jesus. Career ambition for the sake of personal kingdom building, wealth acquisition, making a name for yourself, and selfish objectives with a "Christian label" will not hold up. Hearts *need* to be sold out to Jesus in order for these mantles to be released. God is not seeking perfection. If He was, there would be *no one* available to occupy these places! However, He is seeking perfect obedience and allegiance to the Perfect One. In other words, He is looking for hearts that say a consistent, costly "Yes" to following Jesus. And when you fall, sin, mess up, and miss it, repent and get back up. Keep moving forward.

THE ONE QUALIFICATION FOR "HIGH PLACE" ASSIGNMENTS

God is looking at your surrender, not your gender. Moses argued with God, attempting to convince the One who called him how unqualified he was for the assignment. I believe these silly arguments continue to this very day. Why? Our natural minds reject the call and assignment of God. It's too large. It's impossible. "I've never read about a *woman* who has done this before!" Sadly, for the daughters of God, there has been a great deal of falsity to reject in terms of lies that have been propagated, listing every reason you, as a woman, are not qualified to be a reformer in your generation. Don't follow Moses' example.

Remember, God doesn't write history through people based on their gender; He shapes history through people based on their *surrender.* He is not threatened by our shortcomings, mistakes, or even sins. He is not concerned about our lack of ability or influence. None of these apparent disadvantages motivate God. Try as you might, you cannot talk God out of using you, especially based on your gender.

> *The eyes of the Lord search the whole earth in order to strengthen those whose hearts are fully committed to him* (2 Chronicles 16:9, NLT).

His eyes are looking throughout the earth, seeking the heart that is *fully committed to Him.* The King James Bible calls this a *perfect* heart. I'm sure that translation of this verse trips people up, as they read it and logically conclude, "I'm not perfect, so I must be unqualified to be one of these people the eyes of the Lord look upon." False. God is not looking for perfect performance; He is looking for perfect surrender and obedience. I know people who are stumbling through obedience and surrender, but they are making forward advancement. Momentum is happening. They trip and fall, yes. They work diligently through deliverance, inner healing, and other such matters, confronting their brokenness. This is a fact of life for every human being who is covered in a suit of flesh. As long as we walk the earth in this "flesh suit," we will be navigating that reality. I repeat, God is not seeking women without fault and flaw; what God is looking for is the heart that says an unqualified, consistent, and costly "Yes" to Him.

GO AND TAKE THE HIGH PLACES!

You have been called for such a time as this. You have been placed on earth at this unique moment in history. You have been entrusted with gifts, talents, and abilities that are not meant to be left dormant or un-accessed. You are equipped for an assignment. Ask the Holy Spirit to show you the assignment you have been called to. You could already be working and operating in the place of your assignment, but perhaps you are not tapping into and releasing the *power* available for your assignment. In other words, there is supernatural wisdom, strategy, and creativity waiting to be accessed in the heavenly realm by you *for* your assignment in the sphere of influence you're currently functioning in (your job, career, school, family, etc.).

The Lord wants His people to *desire* to rise to the high places. Promotion. Advancement. Career ambition. You need to know these are okay. More than okay—when partnering with the Holy Spirit, appropriate career ambition can drive you to a high place of influence where you take Jesus into a "high place."

The ones who rule in the high places control and create the narratives. I believe the Lord wants you, daughter of God—filled with His Spirit and operating in His authority—functioning in the high places of your field so that you control the narrative. You shape the narrative that other people are receiving to be one that's under the influence of the Kingdom.

When narratives and messages being communicated are under the influence of sons and daughters of the

Kingdom, these should begin to take on the character traits of children of the Kingdom.

PROPHETIC WORD ABOUT THE "HIGH PLACE" ASSIGNMENT GOD IS CALLING YOU INTO!

I prophesy that as the Lord is handing out swords and mantles to His daughters, He is positioning them to occupy the high places. He hands out these tools for a job—for an assignment.

I prophesy that your assignments will become increasingly clear to you in the corporate place of encounter and the secret place of intimacy.

As the church experiences an increased Holy Spirit reformation, you will come to experience more and more corporate encounters with the Presence of the Spirit. These will be Moses encounters—moments at the "burning bush" when you will receive a profound touch by the fire of God and a reformational calling by the voice of God.

Likewise, you can/will have these same encounters in the "secret place," where it's just you and the Holy Spirit— no one else. The two common denominators, though, that will give you clarity on your assignment and activate you to fulfill it will be the *fire* and the *voice*. The fire of Holy Spirit encounter and the voice that speaks in the encounter. Pay attention! I pray for open and receptive spiritual ears in the days ahead.

I break off the limitations that would try to prevent you from *seeing* your assignment and calling.

Daughter of God, don't simply look at the women who have done, or are doing, what you believe God is calling you to do. For many of the women operating in leadership today, at one point in history there was a forerunner. There was a pioneer who broke something open so that other women could follow—other women could say to themselves, "If she could do *that*, so can I." Remember, at one point in time only *men* could fulfill that assignment.

I sense the Holy Spirit saying that it's very, very good to have positive women role models, both in life and in career aspirations. But I sense that in this urgent hour, God is going to be calling forth prophetic trailblazers. Daughters who will break the mold for the Kingdom of God and, through their examples, call forth to their generation and coming generations, saying, "You can do it too!"

Don't simply look at what women have done; look at what *people* have done. Don't explore the history books, looking for a woman who has done what the Spirit of God is birthing in your heart. Simply look for the yielded vessel who said "Yes" to God and shaped history. If God has given you an assignment out of the fire of encounter, your job is *not* to disqualify yourself—your job is to say "Yes!"

Don't fall into the trap of comparison—specifically, comparing yourself to other women who are doing/not doing what you sense a call to do. Remember, the call of God is not based on gender, but it's based on surrender. So look through the pages of history and the periodicals of this present generation, not for a gender but for those operating in the fields, gifts, callings, and assignments you believe the Lord is awakening in you. It could be a woman;

it could be a man. More than anything, it was a human vessel who said "Yes" to God.

For the *Sovereign Lord* who can do all things seeks a vessel through whom to reach into the earth realm. Yes, He is Lord outside of and over time. He can do all things. And yet He made a sovereign decision to operate in time, in history, on earth, through human vessels. He's seeking a vessel.

Be okay with that! Be okay with the fact that you may *not* read of a woman who is doing what the Lord is calling you to do. It's okay. For I sense that even those occupying a position in the cloud of witnesses, according to Hebrews 12, have faithfully concluded their portion in key Kingdom assignments on earth, but the assignments remain available. The Lord wants you to know that these revolutionary assignments are both available and accessible, and they are not waiting for a gender; they are waiting for a life that shouts out the complete "Yes" of surrender to God, His call, and His Kingdom. In fact, these assignments will continue to remain unfulfilled until "*The kingdom of the world has become the kingdom of our Lord and of his Christ*" (Rev. 11:15). Could it be that when men and women join together in stepping into their assignments, we will see an acceleration in the advancement of God's agenda for the unfolding of history? Whatever your end-times theology might be, the Scripture introduces us to the revolutionary idea of *hastening* the Day of the Lord (see 2 Pet. 3:12). Daughter of God, the Sovereign One has chosen to write you into the very unfolding of history.

Arise and go forth in the authority of your assignment!

NOTE

1. James Bryan Smith, *The Good and Beautiful Life: Putting on the Character of Christ* (Downers Grove: IVP Press), 2009, 19.

HEIDI BAKER

WE ARE IN THE GREATEST TIME OF HISTORY THE WORLD has ever seen. More people are coming to Jesus in this hour, in this age, than ever in the history of the world. It is a tremendous joy to see men and women sharing the Gospel in the marketplace as well as to the unreached people groups of the earth. I am praying for women to rise up in humility and in their giftings and shine.

I am praying for face-to-face encounters with Jesus where they understand who they are, feeling the Father's love embracing their hearts and calling them into their identities in every sphere of society.

Half of the population has felt silenced for a long time, and it is such an encouragement to see women finding their voices. Their sound, their voice, their song is being released all over the planet in every profession.

I see the Lord encouraging them to share in the realm of the church, but to shine wherever they are called to shine.

I love seeing women thriving as professors and in government and as entrepreneurs and also on the mission field. For centuries women have soared on the mission field; it is a place where they felt free. Now it is a time to understand that all of the world, that every single person who doesn't know Jesus, is a field white for harvest.

Women, arise and shine for the glory of God is upon you. It is your season, it is your turn, it is your time. Walk together with faithful men and carry this glorious Gospel. I know that Jesus is calling all of us to have more oil and to be His light on the earth and His salt in the earth. We call half of the population, which is female, to rise up and carry the glory of God!

Chapter Eleven

THE BRIDE WITH A SWORD

Take the mighty razor-sharp Spirit-
sword of the spoken Word of God.
—EPHESIANS 6:17, TPT

IN THE GARDEN OF EDEN, THE CRAFTY SERPENT deceived Eve into forfeiting creation. Adam, Eve—doesn't matter who it was. If Adam was the first person the serpent would have approached, he would have fallen in like manner. The Fall of humanity had little to do with a gender and everything to do with the sin of pride. Mankind then and mankind now, somehow, still think they have an edge on the eternal, perfect, all-knowing God. Foolish, yes, but this propensity comes with the territory of being flesh and blood creatures with a free will.

While many inappropriately target Eve and thus make cases against women in leadership using Eve's yielding to temptation as a faulty example, I want to encourage you to see past what fell and see what's been restored. See past what was lost to what has been renewed. Even though the earth is still adversely impacted by the Fall, there is a new species being born into the planet day after day.

> *Therefore, if anyone is in Christ, he is a new creation. The old has passed away; behold, the new has come* (2 Corinthians 5:17).

As new creations, you have the anointing and authority to bring what you have into collision with the *old creation* and witness transformation take place.

Woman of God, you are a temple of the Holy Spirit. You are a tabernacle, a dwelling place of God on the earth. This means that as a new creation, the One who lives inside of you wants to move *through you* so that things that are broken, sick, and dying can be fixed, healed, and living! The New Creation is meant to come into contact with the *old creation* so that the old can begin to look like the new. This is why creation is groaning. It's not longing for the return of Jesus, per se; it's longing for the revealing of the sons (and daughters) of God.

> *The entire universe is standing on tiptoe, yearning to see the unveiling of God's glorious sons and daughters!* (Romans 8:19, TPT)

The whole of creation is awaiting the emergence of *the new creation*. And remember, the only thing that Scripture describes as a "new creation" is redeemed humanity. I believe for true transformation to take place in the earth— for the bride of Christ, the church, to have the fullness of redemptive impact on creation—both men and women need to embrace identity and assume position. Only when sons and daughters embrace identity as new creations will the old creation receive what it's crying out for—a people who carry redemptive solutions and power. One of the primary ways that power is released by the children of God is through their voice.

Don't be surprised, then, that the enemy wants to silence your voice. If the devil can silence the daughters, then the collective Ekklesia is not operating on all four cylinders. There is a deficit. Earlier in the book, I stressed how sons *and* daughters are called to prophesy. Without the daughters releasing their prophetic voice, the Bride of Christ is muted compared to what it could and should be.

While all women are not called to the five-fold ministry office of prophet (although I see a significant acceleration of women prophets, apostles, pastors, evangelists, and teachers in the body of Christ), all women are indwelt by the prophetic Holy Spirit. Thus, you can *all prophesy!* The Spirit within you is the manifestation or fulfillment of what Moses yearned for in his day: "*I wish that all the Lord's people were prophets and that the Lord would put his Spirit on them!*" (Num. 11:29, NIV). Moses was operating as a prophet while making this utterance, for the Acts 2 outpouring of the Spirit made this a reality—sons and daughters could now prophesy, for they had the Spirit of the Lord inside of them!

In Eden, we literally hear the earth crumble under the weight of the serpent's words to the woman: *"But the serpent said to the woman, 'You will not surely die. For God knows that when you eat of it your eyes will be opened, and you will be like God, knowing good and evil'"* (Gen. 3:4-5). His deception plus her agreement placed the planet under a curse. Again, we need to stop focusing on the gender of the human culprit. Yes, Eve was a woman, but her gender is irrelevant when it comes to analyzing the reason behind the Fall. It was deception. The devil spoke, a human being listened and agreed with his lies, and thus the results were catastrophic.

Yet, I believe the Lord Jesus Christ reversed what took place in the Garden! There was deception that produced a fall, but I also believe there was a reversal that took place at the cross of Calvary that produced a restoration. While we have yet to see the ultimate consummation of this divine reversal take place as the Second Coming of the Messiah, while we live in the "now," let's focus on how much of the "not yet" we can enforce. I use the "now and not yet" language because of the theological tension many point out that we are living in concerning the coming Kingdom of God. It's coming now, and it's coming "not yet." In other words, there is a measure it's coming in right now, in this life, and yet there are other measures of the Kingdom that will come and manifest in fullness in the "not yet," thus pointing to a future end-times scenario.

I'm utterly convinced, woman of God, Jesus wants you to focus on how much of the "not yet" you can bring into the "now." Time after time, when Jesus' disciples got antsy and asked questions about "not yet" items such as when the Kingdom would be fully established, or when He would return, Jesus would always divert the conversation to what they had been granted in the "now."

Consider the conversation that the disciples tried to engage Jesus in following His resurrection:

> *Every time they were gathered together, they asked Jesus, "Lord, is it the time now for you to free Israel and restore our kingdom?" He answered, "The Father is the one who sets the fixed dates and the times of their fulfillment. You are not permitted to know the timing of all that he has prepared by his own authority. But I promise you this—the Holy Spirit will come upon you and you will be filled with power. And you will be my messengers to Jerusalem, throughout Judea, the distant provinces—even to the remotest places on earth!"* (Acts 1:6-8, TPT)

Our focus should not be on the "fixed dates and times of their fulfillment," but rather on being stewards of the *promise* that the Day of Pentecost made available. This is the promise of the Holy Spirit.

The voice of the woman who agreed with the lies of the serpent has now been anointed to prophesy the truth of the Kingdom. Because of the Holy Spirit living within you, you are a living, breathing reversal of what took place in the Garden of Eden. Yes, I recognize that the ultimate manifestation and fulfillment of what God spoke following the Fall was fulfilled in Jesus, the One who crushed the head of the serpent for all time. And yet, though the serpent is indeed crushed and Scripture makes a definitive case for the defeat of Satan, the fact remains that a defeated foe is prowling like a roaring lion seeking whom he may devour (see 1 Pet. 5:8). The defeated foe continues to engage the bride of Christ in warfare. As many have commented, we are not fighting for victory; we are fighting from victory. In spiritual warfare, there should be no question about whether or not the bride of Christ will triumph. She is already triumphant—she simply needs to enforce this triumph. This will only happen to the degree that both the sons and daughters of God are wielding the sword of the Spirit by declaring the word of the Lord!

What happens when the voice of the *woman*, the voice of the bride, agrees with the voice of the Bridegroom?

What happens when the opposite of Eden takes place, and rather than partnering with the voice of Satan the woman speaks back, following the example of the Lord Jesus?

In Eden, she didn't speak to the serpent. But now, her voice roars with authority!

Daughter of God, you have been authorized to speak back to the serpent, Satan.

You've been anointed to speak on behalf of the Savior Jesus!

Bride of Christ, you have been anointed to wield the sword of the Spirit as you prophesy. Your words carry the weight of Heaven as you declare forth what He is already saying.

In the spirit, I see women arising in this hour, speaking with an unusual authority. I see the voices of women being catalytic in ending and cancelling assignments of Satan. I see the words of women cutting through gross and thick plots of darkness, actually exposing schemes like sex trafficking, terrorism, corruption, and all manners of evil that are taking place in the hidden places.

This is not to say that men will have an inferior voice; that's not at all the case. I just see that the voice of the woman will wield a sword of supernatural authority unlike ever before.

I see both men and women of God, fathers and mothers—generals of the faith—seeing the anointing on these emerging women, especially young women. Youth. Teens. Young adults. I see a boldness and courage on these young ones that, if mentored and discipled, will release demonstrations of the Kingdom that the planet has yet to see. I see a fierceness rising up in the daughters of God. This fierceness will not replace the compassion and nurturing that women are often recognized for; but it will compliment it. This fierceness will be prophetic in nature, and I believe will be the result of impartation from the Lion of Judah Himself.

When daughters arise alongside the sons and both wield the sword of the Spirit by prophesying, I believe the planet will witness the emergence of a bride that actually pushes back the influence of darkness!

The serpent rightly fears the brightness of your rising!

Oh let it be that in this hour we would witness the manifestation of the prophetic pronouncement of God Himself in the book of Genesis:

> *The Lord God said to the serpent, "Because you*
> *have done this, cursed are you above all livestock*
> *and above all beasts of the field; on your belly*
> *you shall go, and dust you shall eat all the days*
> *of your life. I will put enmity between you and*
> *the woman, and between your offspring and*
> *her offspring; he shall bruise your head, and you*
> *shall bruise his heel"* (Genesis 3:14-15).

The rightful place of the enemy is described here—his head bruised under the triumphant feet of the woman's offspring, his authority crushed, his kingdom in shambles, and his influence broken. The King James Version specifically identifies this Victorious One as the "seed of the woman." Clearly, this points to Messiah Jesus. And yet, I would suggest that Jesus continues to exercise triumph over the serpent, even today, through a people who are filled with Him and thus called to enforce His victory. These would be the spiritual offspring of God—sons and daughters.

Daughter of God, it's time for you to *arise!* I want to conclude by presenting to you Paul's Ephesians 1 prayer from *The Passion Translation*:

> *I pray that you will continually experience the*
> *immeasurable greatness of God's power made*
> *available to you through faith. Then your lives*
> *will be an advertisement of this immense power*
> *as it works through you! This is the mighty power*
> *that was released when God raised Christ from*
> *the dead and exalted him to the place of highest*
> *honor and supreme authority in the heavenly*
> *realm! And now he is exalted as first above*

*every ruler, authority, government, and realm
of power in existence! He is gloriously enthroned
over every name that is ever praised, not only in
this age, but in the age that is coming!*

*And he alone is the leader and source of every-
thing needed in the church. God has put everything beneath the authority of Jesus Christ and
has given him the highest rank above all others.
And now we, his church, are his body on the earth
and that which fills him who is being filled by it!*
(Ephesians 1:19-23, TPT)

The One living inside of you has filled you with power,
mighty power. Furthermore, He is not only inside of you,
but you are in Him. Christ in you, the hope of glory is
a revelation of the indwelling Presence of the Spirit. You
inside of Christ is an unveiling of your position and
authority. Christ in you speaks of power; you in Christ
speaks of authority.

Daughter, if you are *in Christ*, where is He? After all,
where He is will be where you are, because you are a joint-
heir with Him.

Lift your eyes and see the Son of God *as He* is! He
occupies the place of *"highest honor and supreme authority in the heavenly realm."* You are seated with Christ Jesus
in that heavenly realm. This is not some position you are
trying to attain; this is where you operate from currently.
Jesus' blood was the payment rendered that made it possible for you to occupy this realm and operate from there.
No, a sinful human being cannot possibly be in Christ

and thus have Christ in them. But you are a new creation, remember?

This is why Paul prayed that our spiritual eyes would be open to these realities and that we would receive a spirit of wisdom and revelation in the knowledge of Jesus. First and foremost, may your unending life quest be to simply behold the Son of God as He is. Not because you want a blessing. Not because you need something. Not because He heals, delivers, provides, and grants miracles. Not because He is the key to *this* or the secret to *that*. Jesus is your passion because, quite simply, there is no one like Him. You love Him *for Him*. May Jesus always be first.

But know this. When you truly see Jesus as He is and where He is, then and only then will you be able to discover where you are. Remember what the apostle John noted: *"as he is, so are we in this world"* (1 John 4:17, KJV). Consider how *The Passion Translation* interprets this phrase: *"all that Jesus now is, so are we in this world."* Powerful! Behold Jesus, and you will see who you are in this world—because you are *in Christ*.

Now arise, daughter of God!

Arise, dreamer and creator—dream with God and create with the Holy Spirit!

Arise, mother and wife—raise world-changers and walk in intimacy with history-makers!

Arise, entrepreneur and marketplace innovator—unleash your career ambition, not for selfish gain but for Kingdom influence!

Arise, inventor—hear from Heaven and release the ideas and inventions that display Kingdom glory and author new solutions!

Arise, architect—author new designs that you receive from dreams and visions!

Arise, doctor, nurse, and surgeon—manifest Jehovah Rapha, the Lord who heals!

Arise, psychologist and counselor—prophetically speak into the darkest of troubles and offer hope.

Arise, teacher, principal, and educator—you have the authority to place the very atmosphere and next-gen leaders you have been assigned to under the influence of the Spirit's Presence!

Arise, actor, director, writer—invade media by being a Kingdom renaissance woman.

Arise, producer and shareholder—fund projects that catalyze Kingdom movements.

Arise, pastor and ministry leader—if you are anointed to preach, teach, and lead, step out and boldly steward the call of God on your life!

Arise and shine,

Your light has come, daughter of God.

The glory of the Lord has risen upon you!

Afterword

A Prophetic Reflection

Lana Vawser

*There is a great outpouring of the revelation
of His love upon the daughters of God that
is going to bring the greatest manifestation
of freedom they have ever known!*

THE LORD HAS BEEN SPEAKING TO ME SO MUCH ABOUT "outpouring." We are truly moving into some of the greatest days of seeing the Spirit of God poured out upon the earth.

As I have sat with the Lord, the Lord spoke to me that there is a great outpouring of the revelation of His love upon His daughters in this season that is going to bring them the greatest manifestation of freedom they have ever known.

So many daughters, so many women, have been caged, chained, and contained by so many things for so long. This is a season of great awakening upon His daughters and calling forth the warrior within them. Awakening them to their identity and their authority that has always been theirs in Him.

FEAR NO MORE

The Lord has been showing me so many "lids" that were placed upon many women through lies, through mindsets, through woundings, through things of the past, through words spoken over themselves, words spoken over them by others, disappointment and many other things.

One major lid the Lord showed me in this season was the *lid of fear*. I saw so many women have lived caged under the lid of *fear* for *so long* and many have spent their whole lives pushing in, pressing in, and standing against this fear.

The Lord showed me that this spirit of fear has assaulted so many women, so many of His daughters for so long, and in the assault, they have lost their vision, they have lost their passion, they have lost their voice. They have felt disorientated and contained.

But I heard the Lord say "The time has come now for *all of that* to *change*. There is a great outpouring of the revelation of My love upon My daughters that is going to leave them completely undone and changed by unconditional love."

SO INTENSE, SO FIERCE, SO GENTLE, SO POWERFUL, SO ALL-CONSUMING WILL THE FIRE OF HIS LOVE BE

The great outpouring of the love of Jesus that is being poured out upon the daughters of God is so intense, it is so fierce, yet so gentle, yet so powerful, yet so all-consuming that it is leaving the daughters of God forever changed. There have been so many crying out for freedom, so many crying out for healing, so many crying out for restoration, and the Lord has heard. The encounters with the fire of His love are not to be feared, but embraced. They will remove *all* roots of fear. *All* roots of fear; *all* landing places of fear; *all* the places where fear has stolen, killed, and destroyed from the daughters of God—*removed*. The barren places are suddenly coming to life. Where fear has hindered fruitfulness, suddenly gardens of fruitfulness are exploding all around as the revelation of His love brings life, resurrection, and increase.

The Lord showed me that the encounters with the fire of His love upon the daughters of God in this season are *branding encounters*. They are encounters that will leave them *forever marked* by the love of God. Encounters where they will look back on them for years to come as the encounters that changed their life, changed their direction, changed their current situation, broke the chains, and catapulted them further into their destiny and engaging with the realms of influence the Lord had given them.

VOICES RESTORED AND CREATIVITY REBIRTHED

The Lord showed me that because of the intense spirit of fear that has come against the daughters of God, many have lost their voice. They have lost their song. Many don't know what their "song" is anymore. These powerful encounters with the fire of His love, these encounters with the revelation of His love, will *suddenly* restore their voices. The lies suddenly break off and the muzzles over mouths are suddenly removed. Where fear has tried to muzzle them and muffle their sound and their voice, in these powerful encounters with the fire of His love a boldness and conviction to speak and release their songs upon the earth is being released with such love and an unwavering resolve. Such beautiful confidence in who they are in Him and the song He has given them to release into the world in their spheres of influence. They are no longer compromised by fear, insecurity, or comparison but fueled by the fire of His love and revelation that what they carry and have to release is powerful and unique.

REVIVAL OF CREATIVITY

The Lord showed me that fear has caused a miscarriage of creative birthing in the lives of many of the daughters of God. I saw the words "I can't" written all over their hearts. I saw these powerful encounters with the fire of His love *changing the script.* The scripts that have been written over hearts of many daughters of God are *so opposite* to what He says and *so* opposite to His plans and purposes for their lives (see Jer. 29:11). In these powerful encounters with the love of God, the fire of His truth is *rewriting* the script and *reviving and unlocking* a great revival of creativity.

The "I can'ts" were being rewritten by His love to "*In Him, I can!*"

I heard the Holy Spirit say "*Nothing has been lost and nothing has been missed.*"

As I heard that I wondered what He meant. I had seen a miscarriage of creativity in the spirit that has happened for many daughters of God. Instantly, He spoke to me:

> *What seems impossible to you is never impossible to God!* (Matthew 19:26, TPT)

Then I was suddenly surrounded by Ezekiel 37 and the passage of the dry bones. Prophesying to the dry bones.

The Lord showed me that He is prophesying over the dry bones of creativity in the lives of His daughters and breathing upon them again, and they are beginning to rattle. They are beginning to come to life. They are beginning to show signs of life again.

I prophesy over the creativity He has placed within you: "You are coming to life in Jesus' name! I prophesy the resurrection power of Jesus Christ is falling upon the creativity that has been miscarried and speak reversal. I speak life. I speak and decree that the Lord is restoring to you now not only the creativity that was lost, but double portion *restoration* of creativity is being birthed in you and through you in Jesus' name."

Nothing has been lost and nothing has been missed, because He is redeeming it. He is restoring it, and not only that, He is adding increase to it.

WATCH THE PIONEERING CREATIVITY THAT WILL BE RELEASED THROUGH MY DAUGHTERS IN THIS SEASON

I heard Him say, "Watch the pioneering creativity that is going to be released through My daughters in this season."

The Lord showed me that as the awakening and revival of creativity is happening, a pioneering spirit is falling upon the daughters of God. Releasing the creative expression of Heaven through them in their sphere of influence.

The Lord spoke again:

"Watch as what has never been done is about to be done as My creative expression through My daughters is released."

I saw the daughters of God rising up in such powerful ways in their spheres of influence with incredible creative wisdom, strategy, invention, blueprints, and insight in their spheres of influence. Things that have never been done, things that were said never could be done, and new pathways are being forged by His wonder women unafraid to pioneer and build for His Kingdom in *their* creative lane.

I saw such a spearheading happening in the body of Christ and in the world through the daughters of God right now, forerunning and releasing a new and creative demonstration of the heart of God and the good news of Jesus Christ into their spheres of influence.

RELEASE OF AN IMPARTATION OF FIRE FOR FIRST LOVE ENCOUNTERS IN THE BODY OF CHRIST

In these powerful encounters with the fire of His love, I saw where *fear* has kept many women hidden and hindered their relationship with the Lord, where the fox of fear has hindered the vineyard of love (see Song 2:15, TPT). Now they are *suddenly* removed and restoration of intimacy with Jesus is taking place, and a return to the first love is happening. Where fear has hindered communion, friendship with Jesus, and encounter, the fire of His love is falling so powerfully in a whole new season of *"first love fire encounters,"* bringing a deeper place of intimacy and divine dance with the Beloved than they have ever known.

Through these encounters I saw beautiful impartations of fire being released to them. They were left so undone, so wrecked by His love, so changed by the revelation of His love, goodness, kindness, and who they are in Him that wherever they went they released the fire of His love, releasing impartation for others to encounter Jesus as the first love. I saw it happening in the church and I saw it happening outside the church.

He whispered again: "What I am doing in and through My daughters is a major key in this season of harvest."

The sense surrounded me so strongly that there is a mighty move of the Spirit of God through the daughters of God rising up to stand alongside the men of God, and they will usher in an incredible harvest and mighty move of the Spirit of God upon the earth unlike we have ever seen.

These encounters with the fire of God so powerful were branding Song of Songs 8:6-7 upon the hearts of the daughters of God:

> *Fasten me upon your heart as a seal of fire forevermore. This living, consuming flame will seal you as my prisoner of love. My passion is stronger than the chains of death and the grave, all consuming as the very flashes of fire from the burning heart of God. Place this fierce, unrelenting fire over your entire being. Rivers of pain and persecution will never extinguish this flame. Endless floods will be unable to quench this raging fire that burns within you. Everything will be consumed. It will stop at nothing as you yield everything to this furious fire until it won't even seem to you like a sacrifice anymore* (TPT).

The daughters of God are rising up, carrying this fire. That deep place of yieldedness, unquenchable, raging fire is so all consuming that they are left sealed forevermore by the flames of His love, leading them to such a *joy* in surrender. The message that brands their hearts in these encounters with His fire is the same message and fire that will be released *through them*.

EVERYTHING IS CHANGING

Daughters of God, many of you have been captive for so long to fear. This is not your inheritance. This is not your portion. In this season, that changes. Everything is changing.

For God will never give you the spirit of fear,
but the Holy Spirit who gives you mighty power,
love, and self-control (2 Timothy 1:7, TPT).

You have been captive to fear, and the wrong scripts have been branded upon your heart and locked over your mind by its evil, death-giving whispers. But I prophesy over you a season of encountering the fire of His love, being a prisoner only to His love is upon you. A season of *whispers* is upon you, but it is hearing the *whispers* of *love*, the whispers of His heart in greater ways. You will carry the secrets of His heart as you linger with Him. The whispers that tormented you will be no more. Now you will know whispers that ignite the fire of His love with such increase, creativity, and vision within you. You will know at a deeper level the whispers that lead you to life, and these whispers will impart such fire in your bones you will not be able to keep from speaking. Your hearts will burn as you have been with Him and as you hear Him speak clearer than ever.

WHERE YOUR VISION WAS STOLEN, NOW YOU SHALL SEE FURTHER THAN EVER

Where fear has stolen your vision, now you shall see further than ever. I prophesy a season of *sight* over you. Holy Spirit, awaken their sight to see, as You see, the areas where sight has been stolen. Lord, open their eyes to see further than they have seen before. Many of you are about to see things in the spirit that are not even yet imagined in the natural. The Lord is going to open up His Word to you so deeply and show you such revelation that you will now understand why there has been such a battle over your life to steal your vision.

Daughters, this is your time to be free from the chains of fear that have entangled you and know the love of God—the beautiful, all-consuming fire of His love like never before.

You're about to be branded.

Wrecked by His love.

Consumed by His delight of you.

Burning with His flames of love for you that will birth an unshakeable resolve within you.

The spirit of fear has been given its eviction notice.

"Forever changed" will be the testimony that flows from your mouth from these encounters. You will look back on these encounters forever.

Partner with Him, agree with His invitation.

Fire of God, *come!*

About the Authors

PATRICIA KING

Patricia King is a respected apostolic minister of the Gospel, successful business owner, and an inventive entrepreneur. She is an accomplished itinerant speaker, author, television host, media producer, and ministry network overseer who has given her life fully to Jesus Christ and to His Kingdom's advancement in the earth. She is the founder of Patricia King Ministries and co-founder of XPmedia.com.

LARRY SPARKS

Larry Sparks is publisher for Destiny Image (destinyimage.com), a Spirit-filled publishing house pioneered by Don Nori Sr. in 1983 with a mandate to *publish the prophets*. Larry is fueled by a vision to help the church community create space for the Holy Spirit to move in freedom, power, and revival fire, providing every believer with an opportunity to have a life-changing encounter in the Presence of God. In addition to publishing, Larry is a regular contributor to *Charisma* magazine; he conducts seminars on revival; hosts regional *Renewing South Florida* gatherings;, and has been featured on Sid Roth's *It's Supernatural,* TBN, CBN, the ElijahList, and Cornerstone TV. He earned a Master of Divinity from Regent University and enjoys life in Texas with his beautiful wife and beloved daughter (lawrencesparks.com).

Experience a personal revival!

Spirit-empowered content from today's top Christian authors delivered directly to your inbox.

Join today!
lovetoreadclub.com

Inspiring Articles

Powerful Video Teaching

Resources for Revival

Get all of this and so much more, e-mailed to you twice weekly!

LOVE TO READ CLUB

by **D DESTINY IMAGE**

Printed in Great Britain
by Amazon

35766653R00112